GUITAR

FOR

ABSOLUTE BEGINNERS

Published in the United States by NYC Guitar School.

NYC Guitar School
251 West 30th Street
New York, NY 10001

Publisher: Dan Emery
Copy editor: Suzanne Bilyeu
Book design: Chika Azuma
Illustrator: Dan Emery and Alia Madden
Photographer: Woody Quinn, Dan Emery, and Genifer Owen

Paper: Oxford The Holly Hunt Collection, Fired, 100 lb. cover and Cougar Natural Opaque, 60 lb. text
Printing: Peeq Media

ISBN 978-0-9825998-0-8
First edition

Printed and Bound in the United States

Acknowledgements

In 2004, New York City Guitar School consisted of a single room in the Recording and Rehearsal Arts Building on West 30th Street in Manhattan. One door led to the offices of four other businesses. The other led to a shared bathroom. As my students and I moved our guitars aside to allow yet another person to use the facilities, I did not imagine that six years later New York City Guitar School would have over thirty teachers and twenty classrooms in three locations in Manhattan, Brooklyn and Queens, or that thousands of students would learn to play guitar using the curriculum which you now hold in your hands. This would not have happened without the support, involvement and encouragement of hundreds of people.

The heart of a great guitar school is great teachers. Lenny Molotov, Anne Husick, Matt Boas and Suke Cerulo joined the school six years ago and are still teaching spectacular lessons here today. I thank them for forming the core of the most student-centered guitar faculty in America, and for improving this guitar manual by letting me know what did and did not work for their students.

The development of the book has been inseparable from the development of New York City Guitar School itself. This success would not have been possible without the enthusiasm, dedication and leadership of Director Jen Elliott, for which I thank her. I am also thankful to Shane Chapman, who runs Brooklyn Guitar School, where his creativity and hard work have brought this course to hundreds of happy Brooklynites. Appreciation is also due to veteran front desk superstar Genifer Owen for the sweet voice and mind-blowing enthusiasm which have helped many nervous first-time students get off to a successful start in their guitar career.

NYC Guitar School teacher Vince DeMasi generously read and advised me on the material. He also did much of the research on song progressions which you'll see at the end of each lesson, and with his permission I've kept intact some of his text and jokes, especially at the end of lessons 2, 3, 7 and 8. Brooklyn Guitar School teacher Woody Quinn took most of the photos in the book. Work-study student April Koester typed the entire manual three times. Alia Madden (www.avphibes.com) created most of the most striking images in the manual (the not-striking ones are mine). Chika Azuma did the amazing book design. Suzanne Bilyeu edited the material, improving it dramatically despite removing hundreds of my precious exclamation points!!!

The lion's share of the credit goes to the amazing New York City Guitar School Students. Early students Rita Caliendo, Nelson Cheung, Mary Ghiorzi, and Gerry Borrell encouraged me to have a larger vision of the course. Since then, hundreds of students have taken a moment in the lounge, elevator or hallways to say what they liked and disliked about the course. Their support has carried me through days both fair and foul. I can't believe my good fortune to be so constantly surrounded by such wonderful and inspiring people.

Finally, words cannot express my thanks to my wife, Miriam, for her unyielding faith in me.

GUITAR

FOR

ABSOLUTE BEGINNERS

NEW YORK CITY GUITAR SCHOOL

What is the Fundamental Secret of Playing Guitar Successfully?

PERHAPS YOU WANT TO PLAY GUITAR because you really love music, and you want to be able to make beautiful music yourself. Maybe you want to eventually play music with other people, or write your own songs, or play for your toddler—or perhaps you want to be a rock star! All of these and others are fine reasons to play guitar.

Regardless of your particular motivation, let us recognize the one thing that you MUST do on your way to achieving your goals. **To be a guitar player, you must play guitar!** That's right! If you truly want to play guitar, let us understand right now that you are going to have to pick up your guitar, hold it in your hands and play it to the best of your ability. This is called "practicing," and the more often you practice, the more and the sooner you will realize your goal and desire of being a guitar player.

In your studies at New York City Guitar School, you will gain a solid understanding of the habits and techniques necessary for a lifetime of guitar enjoyment and learning. Your teachers will present these powerful ideas to you in a clear and uplifting manner. But as committed and enthusiastic as the teachers at New York City Guitar School are, they will not deserve the credit for your progress. The credit will be all yours; playing guitar is in your hands.

If you will only pick up your guitar and play it regularly, then with the aid of your teachers you will soon be amazing yourself. In fact, I think you will be surprised by how easily and comfortably you will learn. To play guitar with confidence and skill, make a deep and powerful commitment right now to the fundamental secret of playing guitar:

To master guitar playing you must play your guitar!

TO MASTER GUITAR PLAYING YOU MUST PLAY YOUR GUITAR!

CLASS

1

The Fundamental Habits of Great Guitar Players

~ by Dan Emery of NYC Guitar School ©2009 ~

{ *Identifying strings, frets and fingers; the rest stroke; chord diagrams; D and G chords; proper fretting; planting fingers; strumming the optimum number of strings; how to practice. FOR NEXT WEEK, BRING A TUNER TO CLASS. Plus—Great Songs!* }

This is a hands-on lesson, so grab your soon-to-be trusty guitar, sit down and put it right in your lap, with this text on the table, counter or milk crate in front of you. Today you will begin to internalize the habits of a great guitar player!

What is This Thing in My Lap?

It is called a guitar. Since you are now a guitar player, you need to know your way around the guitar, just like an astronaut needs to know which button is which in the space shuttle. So let's learn the PARTS OF THE GUITAR. I **know** that you are eager to cut to the chase and begin playing fun songs—so please read through this section so that you learn the material and you never need to study it again.

Most of the people taking this course have an acoustic guitar at home like the one pictured below. A picture may be worth a thousand words—but actually reaching out and touching something is worth a thousand pictures. So reach out and touch each part of your guitar corresponding to the labeled parts in the pictures below, and clearly recite the name to yourself. If you are playing a classical guitar it will have nylon strings and no pickguard, and if you are playing an electric guitar it will have some electronic parts and controllers, but the essentials will be the same.

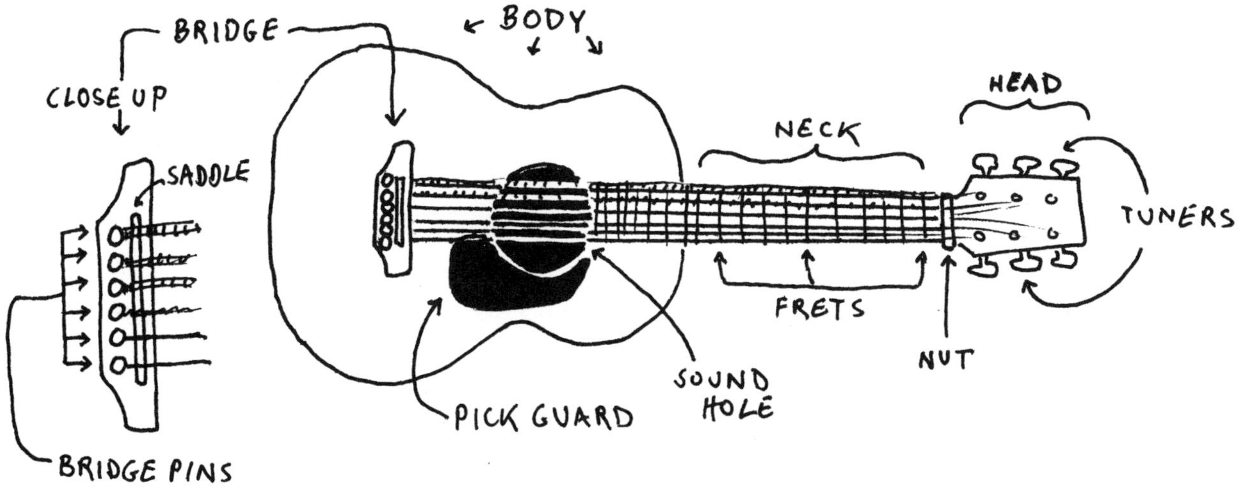

How to Hold the Guitar

We're not learning to play classical guitar in this book, and most players in every other style of music rest the guitar on their thigh. Why don't you do that, and play some experimental-having-no-idea-what-you're-doing guitar for a moment. Let your strumming arm rest on top of the guitar, relax, and imagine yourself playing your favorite song. If you feel a little awkward, that is OK, because after all you've been a guitar player for only four or five minutes.

> **Good Guitar Players Strum Efficiently, Using Rest Strokes.**
>
> When strumming, let your hand drop and brush against the string or strings, coming to a rest against another string or the guitar body.

How to Strum the Guitar Correctly

Right now you are developing habits that will stay with you for many, many years. Doesn't it make sense to develop good habits immediately? In the next lesson we'll start using a pick, but first we want to achieve perfect, beautiful strumming form, and that is best accomplished by spending some time strumming with your thumb using a technique called "the rest stroke." Let the thumb of your strumming hand (i.e. the right hand for right-handers and left hand for left-handers) rest on the thickest string of the guitar, more or less over the sound hole. Be relaxed—let gravity drag some of the weight of your thumb and hand against the string. Emulate the picture below as much as possible:

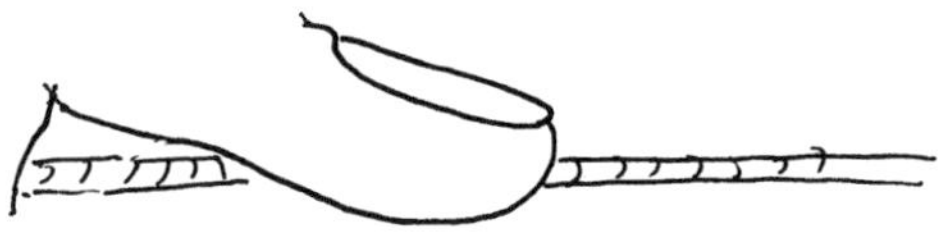

Now, allow gravity to gently pull your thumb down. It will strum the thickest string as it falls to REST against the next string. Here is a picture of the same thumb after strumming the sixth string with a rest stroke:

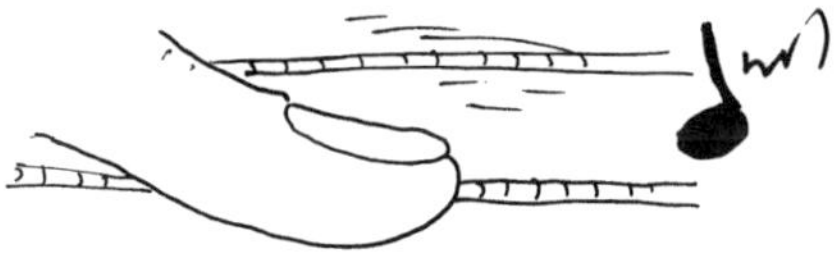

The rest stroke is not only restful and relaxed, but the thumb always comes to a REST on the next string. That's why it is called the rest stroke. Try playing rest strokes on various strings one by one, always with the thumb coming to rest on the next string. When you get to the thinnest string, let your thumb fall against the body of the guitar, as below:

Spend a moment investing in your guitar future by becoming modestly comfortable with rest strokes. Practice playing rest strokes on various strings. Then practice strumming all the strings; your thumb will brush against each string in turn, finishing against the body of the guitar.

By the way, there are two habits to especially avoid in strumming: **Don't** grip the bottom of the guitar with your fingers. **Don't** swoop your hand or thumb out into the air. **Do** play smooth, relaxed efficient rest strokes. Using rest strokes is one of the fundamental habits of a great guitar player.

To Play Guitar, You Must Identify Strings. Here's How:

Strings are numbered from thinnest to thickest—the thinnest string is called the first string, the next thinnest is called the second string, and so on until we get to the thickest string, which is called the sixth string. Remember: **The thinnest string is called the first string.** Learn the string numbers by doing the following exercise—put the thumb of your strumming hand on the 6th (thickest) string and play a rest stroke. Now your thumb is on the 5th string. Play it with a rest stroke. Now find and play the following strings: 4, 3, 2, 1, 6, 1, 5, 2, 3, 4. You now know how to identify strings. Here is a labeled picture:

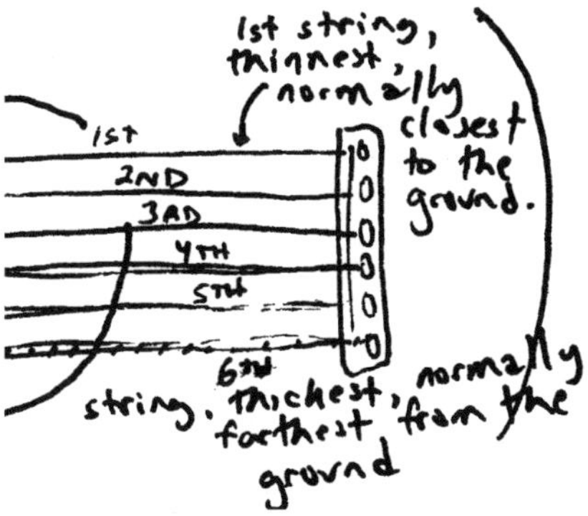

NOTE: THIS IS A NEW, AERIAL VIEW OF THE STRINGS, AS THOUGH THE GUITAR IS SITTING ON YOUR LAP FACING UP.

To Play Guitar, You Must Identify Frets. Here's How:

Now examine this pictograph of the very end of the neck, where it meets the head. Note that the frets are also numbered. The fret closest to the nut is called the first fret; the next one is the second fret and so on. Touch the following frets with any finger you like as an exercise: 1, 2, 3, 4, 2, 1, 3.

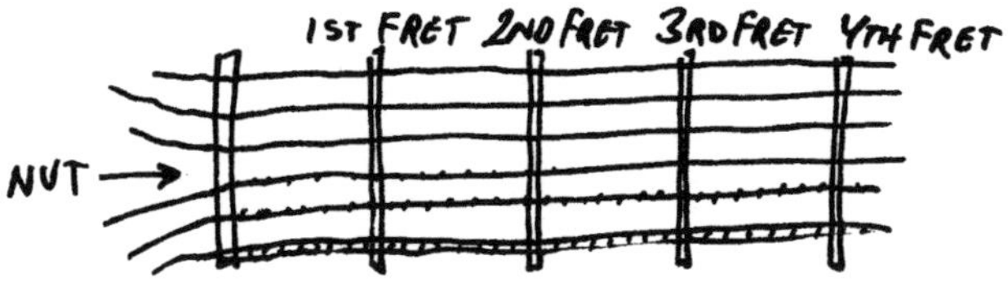

THIS IS AN AERIAL VIEW

Do you see what we've accomplished here? We can now identify any intersection of string and fret on the guitar! Try it. Remember that **the thinnest string is the first string** and locate: the first string at the first fret; the second string at the second fret; the sixth string at the third fret; the fourth string at the first fret; the third string at the fourth fret. Again, remember that **the thinnest string is called the first string.** Good work! You now understand how to locate frets and strings.

Remember, the Thinnest String is the First String and the Thickest String is the Sixth String!

Fret with the Tip of your Finger Almost, but Not Quite, on the Fret!

Use Your Fingertips to Play Clear and Clean Notes

Did you know that fingers might be identified differently when playing different instruments? For example, piano players call their thumb the first finger. But not us guitarists! We call a thumb a thumb, and the index finger is the first finger.

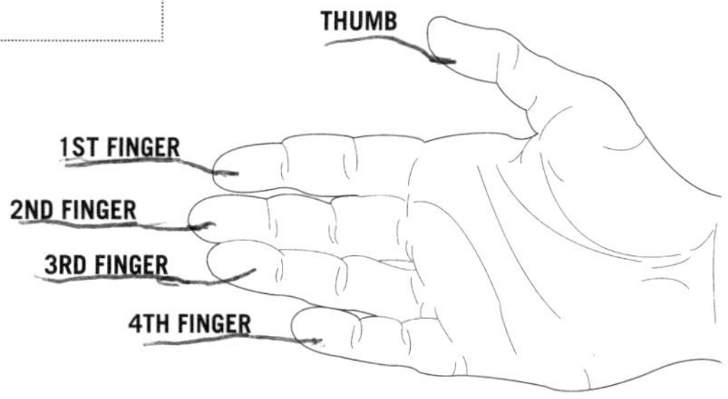

Now try "fretting" a note. Press the tip of your first finger against the first string just behind the first fret ("behind" means on the head side of the fret, not the body side of the fret). Push down until the string is pressed against the fret. Following is a helpful picture. Notice that this guitarist is really using just the fingertip. Keep your thumb behind the neck, providing support for the fingers; the arm is relaxed, elbow near the body.

After you fret the first string at the first fret, put the thumb of your right hand on the first string and strum it with a rest stroke. If you hear a buzzing sound, or a "thunk" instead of a clear note, then everything is proceeding normally! Ask yourself: "Am I using the very tip of my finger?"; "Is my fingertip close to the first fret (but not actually on top of it)?"; "Is my thumb against the back of the neck opposite my first finger?" and "Am I pressing the string down hard enough to press the string against the fret?" Keep trying until you hear your note.

By the way, if your nails are too long, you won't be able to fret clearly. I realize that it really can be a sacrifice to get out the nail clippers and cut them down to size. Just remember that Bonnie Raitt, Ani Difranco and Tracy Chapman cut their nails, and they can play the heck out of the guitar.

Take a moment to fret and strum notes all over the guitar on different strings with different fingertips. Remember to use a beautifully relaxed and efficient rest stroke each time.

Your First Chord

You have learned two vital habits of playing guitar—rest strokes and using your fingertips to hold down the string close to the fret. You are now ready to tease the fingers of your fretting hand into a strange configuration known as a "chord." You can think of a chord as a set of notes that sound good together. Your first chord will be the D major chord, usually just called "D." At first, you may think that D stands for "darn it" or "dang it," but soon you will discover that D stands for "Dy-no-mite!"

Begin making a D chord by putting the first finger of your left hand on the third string at the second fret. This is your **plant** finger. Always when you make a D chord, you will begin with this finger, until that time at which all your fingers will fret the chord simultaneously. Of course, I know that you will remember the fundamental good habits of using your fingertips and playing close to the fret. So put the tip of your first finger on that third string almost but not quite on the second fret and press down.

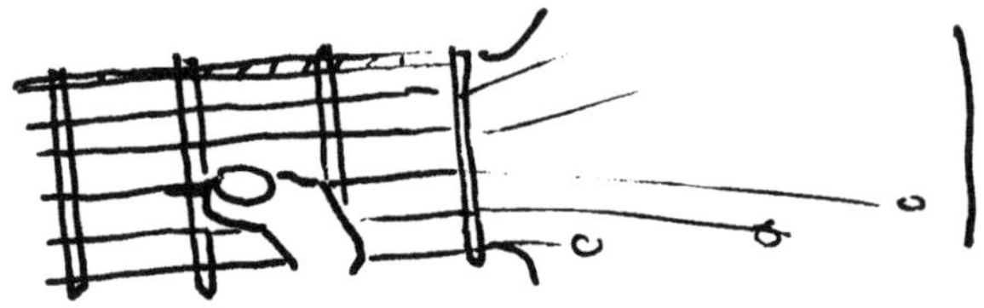

Now in **addition** to your first finger, put your second finger on the first string (thinnest), also at the second fret. Ideally both fingertips should be close to the fret—it may be helpful to turn your hand slightly to accomplish this.

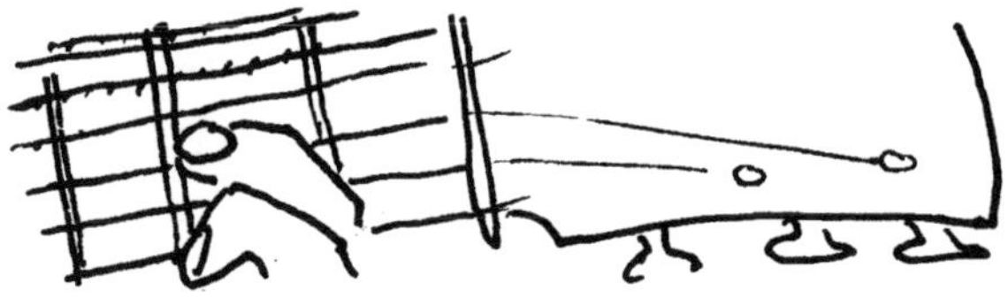

Finally, reach out with the third finger to play the second string at the third fret. Sort of a reach, huh? Do not be dismayed if this seems difficult—remember that every guitarist had to do this for the first time at some point. Press the strings down with all three fingertips.

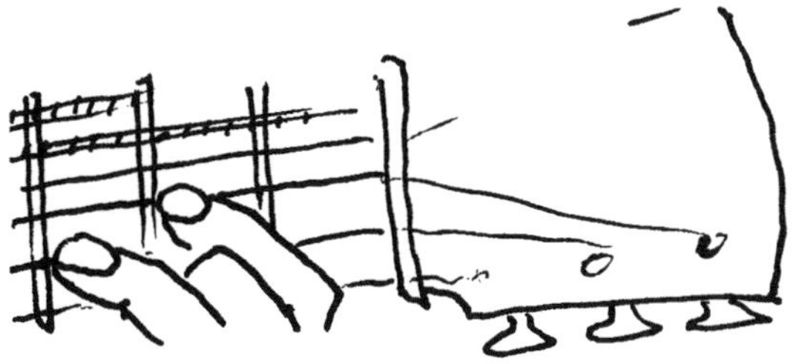

You're now making a D chord! Lift all your fingers up and make a D chord again, one finger at a time. Notice that your fingertips outline a triangle.

Then do it again. And again. And again, again, again, again, again.

Strumming the D Chord

Now rest the thumb of your strumming hand on the fourth string and try an experimental strum or two. Let your thumb fall all the way down to the body of the guitar with each strum.

If each string sounded pristine and clear, you may do a dance of joy. However, if you are like me when I started, or just about everybody else, one, two or even three of the strings made a "buzz" or "thunk" instead of a clear sound. If this is the case, look over at your left hand. Probably one of your fingers is bumping into a string (usually it is the third finger bumping against the first string.)

Here's a chord-troubleshooting checklist:

Are you using your fingertips to fret the chord?
Are you fretting close to (but not on top of) the frets?
Are you pushing the strings against the frets?

Readjust and try again, string by string. Each time you make the D chord, begin with your first fingertip (because it is the plant finger!).

Remember that we seek perfection—but we don't expect it immediately. New guitar players typically need several weeks of practice before their D chord is consistently clear. (But don't wait for perfection—start learning to play songs even if just a couple of strings ring out clearly.)

Please note that ideally, we want to hear not only the three strings that you are holding down with your fingers, but also the fourth string, even though it is open (i.e. unfretted). We DON'T want to hear the fifth and sixth strings—they aren't part of our D chord.

Now, practice making the D chord. The first thing we need to accomplish is a rough familiarity with the chord, so don't worry about how it sounds. Just repeatedly form a D chord by putting the first fingertip down, then the second, then the third, and then a beautiful little strum of the four thinnest strings. Do this for five or 15 minutes, just long enough to begin feeling a little comfortable with the D chord. Then go on to the next section.

Practice Makes Perfect

THE D MAJOR CHORD
Your journey of a thousand songs begins with D.

THE G MAJOR CHORD
Knowing G is an absolute must, because it shows up more often and in more songs than any other chord.

Learning to Read Chord Diagrams

THERE IS A CONVENTIONAL WAY for guitarists to communicate how a chord is played, called a CHORD DIAGRAM.

Remember when we zoomed in on the neck of the guitar when we learned how to identify frets? This is an aerial view. We're looking straight down at the guitar. It is lying on its back.

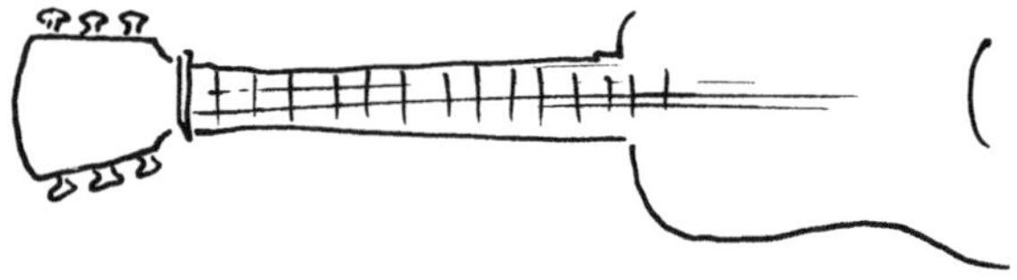

Let's zoom in even more.

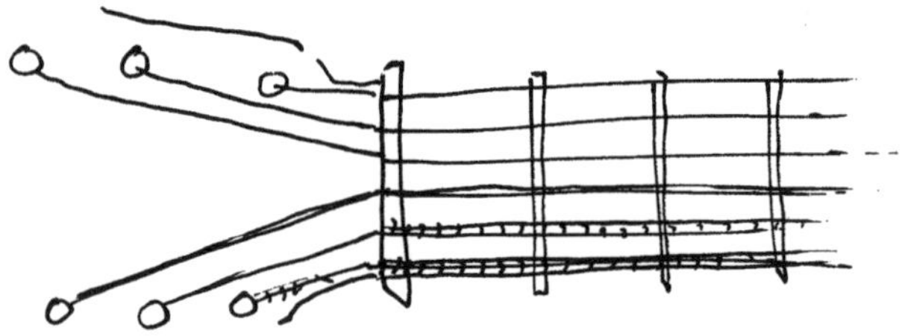

Now let's superimpose the fingertips of a D chord.

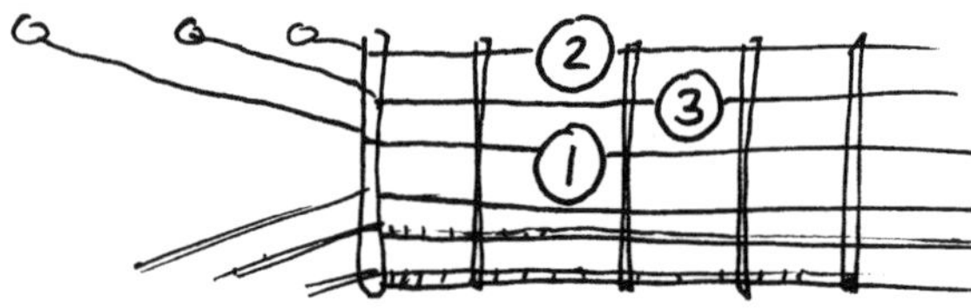

Next, we'll indicate that we're supposed to strum only four strings on this chord by Xing out the strings that we **don't** play (the 5th and 6th strings.) While we're at it, let's make it clear that we **do** play the 4th string, even though we're not fretting it, by placing an "O" for open next to that string.

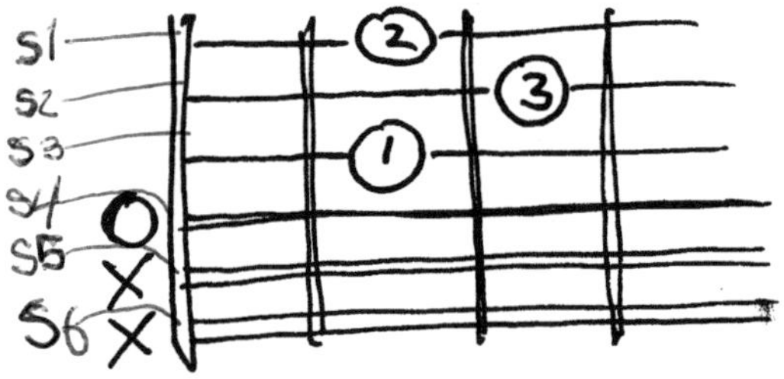

Now, let's turn this picture into a diagram by taking out the head of the guitar, and the extra frets, and by turning the nut and thick strings into just normal lines.

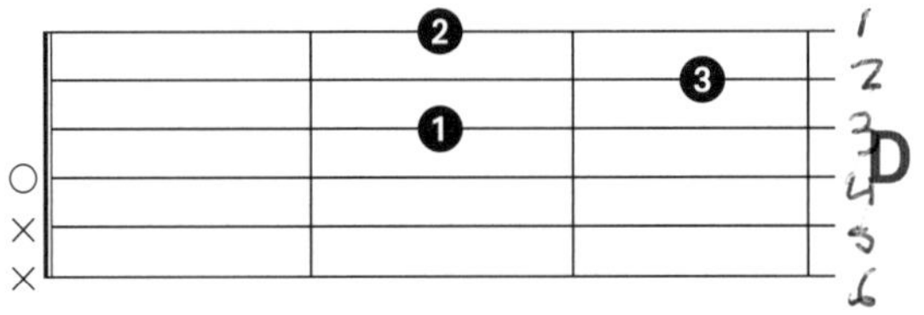

From now on, not only in this course but for the rest of your guitar career, you will be reading and understanding chord diagrams.

The Next Chord: G Major

USE YOUR NEWFOUND chord-diagram reading skills to learn the G major chord. This chord is used more than any other chord in rock and roll.

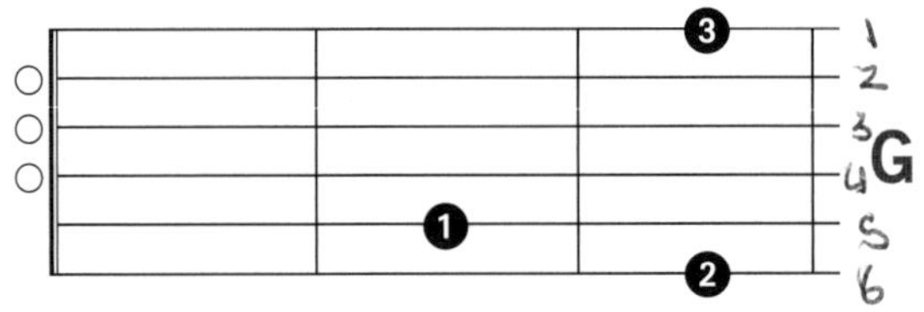

You can think of G standing for "giant" because there is a giant stretch involved. Put down the second finger on the sixth (thickest) string, close to the third fret. This is your **plant** finger. Eventually, all your fingers will make the chord simultaneously, but in the meantime, when playing a G, lead with the second finger, which holds down the most important note in the chord. Remember to fret with your fingertip close to (but not on top of) the fret.

Then put down the third finger on the opposite side of the guitar neck, on the first (thinnest) string, also close to the third fret.

Finally, put down the first finger on the fifth string (next-to-thickest) and close to the second fret. This is sort of a bonus finger—many competent guitarists leave it off.

Again, as you did with the D chord, make a few experimental strums. This time you will strum all six strings. And again, check to avoid those buzzing and thunk-like sounds by asking:

Am I using my fingertips to fret the chord?
Am I fretting close to (but not on top of) the frets?
Am I pushing the strings against the frets?

Take five or ten minutes to achieve a rough familiarity with the G chord. Again, we strive for perfection but we don't expect it immediately. Even though your G chord doesn't yet sound completely clear, when you are moderately confident with the basic shape of it, go on to the next section.

The Most Powerful Chord Exercise of All

BACK IN MY COLLEGE DAYS, I ran track and cross-country for the University of Idaho. I was always trying to find some special way to practice that would give an extra edge, preferably without running eight or ten miles every morning. Once I read an article about a new workout consisting of jumping on and off a box, and I excitedly ran to see Ken, the trainer. "Ken," I yelled, "I'm gonna jump up on a box and then back down for 45 minutes every morning so that I'll be a better long-distance runner."

Ken looked at me for a moment, then said, "Dan, jumping on and off a big wooden box might help you to become a better box jumper, but if you want to be a better long-distance runner, why don't you go run eight or ten miles?"

So it is with guitar playing. Drills are great, but the best way to get good at playing guitar is to play guitar—so let's begin! The single most powerful thing you can do **right now** to become a better guitar player is to change back and forth between a D and a G chord incessantly. You see, making a chord isn't the hard part of guitar playing—**changing chords** in the middle of a song is the hard part. So get ready, and change back and forth between D and G. Take your time. Remember:

ON THE D CHORD—Lead with your first finger...use your fingertips...strum four strings.

ON THE G CHORD—Lead with your second finger...use your fingertips...strum six strings.

It seems to me that most people need to play this change somewhere between 400 and 900 times to feel really confident with it—so do your rock-star guitar-playing self a great favor and change chords relentlessly over the next week! Change chords while listening to music, watching TV, talking on the phone, at breakfast, while riding your unicycle.

Questions and Answers for Beginning Guitarists

Q: *My fingertips hurt—is that okay?*
A: That's okay. As long as they aren't actually bleeding or blistering, there is no problem. Jimi Hendrix, Eric Clapton and Sheryl Crow all had sore fingertips when they started playing guitar! The only way to make your fingertips stop hurting is to play enough for your fingers to toughen up—usually this takes three or four weeks of steady practice. If your fingers do blister, **you might be** practicing too much, but more likely your guitar is a bad instrument, or you're playing with way too much force, or both. Remember, almost every challenge in guitar is solved with good form, not brute force.

Q: *My wrist hurts—is that okay?*
A: No, that is not okay. Fingertip pain is a pain in a fleshy bit of your finger, which soon adapts. Wrist pain can be in your tendons and joint and can get worse with time. And when pain gets worse, it is hard to practice relentlessly. Avoid wrist pain by keeping your fretting wrist straight, as in the following sketches:

Now, some people may tell you that the bent-wrist method is more proper, especially trained classical-guitar players. But trained classical guitarists have been building up their strength for years—and besides, they usually aren't playing chords. Also, they are holding their guitars almost vertically on their laps. On the other hand, look at just about any accomplished rock, folk, country, pop or alternative player, and you'll see that their wrists are relatively straight. So let's be like them! In fact, if you have to choose between a clear-sounding chord and a healthy wrist position, be healthy! Chord clarity will come with time and practice. In the unlikely, but not unheard of, event that your wrists, joints or tendons are extremely sore after a week of practice, bring your guitar in so that your teacher can check it for playability, and ask for advice on your playing.

I've included charts and sketches below to help you determine if your pain is okay, or not okay.

DON'T DO THIS—the bent wrist causes wrist pain

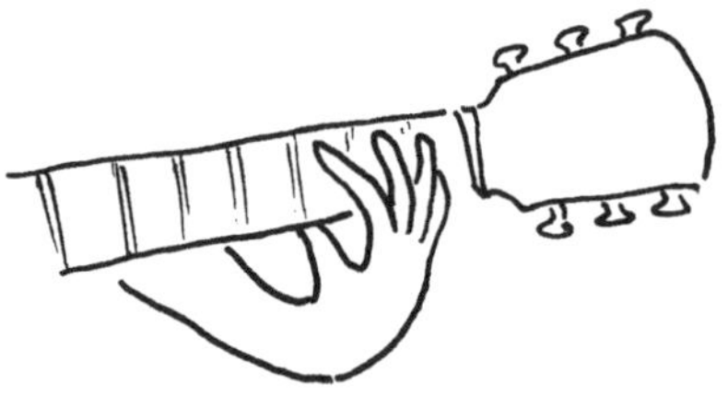

DO THIS—a relatively straight wrist is good.

TYPE OF PAIN	OKAY PAIN	NOT-OKAY PAIN
Fleshy finger pad soreness		
Muscle soreness		
Wrist pain		
Joint/tendon pain		
Bleeding fingers		

How to Practice Guitar Effectively

1. Practice Accurately.

When you practice playing your guitar, you are literally creating new pathways in your neurons, which are cells in your brain. As you practice your D chord over and over, for example, you deepen and widen this pathway and make new connections. For the beginning guitarist, a D chord will consist of several different actions in your mind, like this set of commands to your brain and body:

You: "Hey brain and fingers–give me a D chord!"

Your Brain: "OK, let's see here, uh, first I'll put your first finger down on the third string, then I'll, uh, remember that the strings are counted from thin to thick, and then, uh, I'll remember that I need to use the fingertip, OK, now let's go with the second finger—I mean, fingertip—and I'll make sure that the fingertip is close to the fret... so far so good, now for the third fingertip, and I'm not forgetting to keep your fingers coming in all pointy...there you go, a D chord—oh, wait, I almost forgot that I need to have my right hand strum, uh, five, no, four strings!"

It is amazing that we can do this difficult and complex task at all...but as you practice and practice, your brain learns the sequence. So after a month of regular practice your conversation with your brain looks more like this.

You: "Gimme a D!"

Your Brain: BAM! (Your brain has made a D chord and is ready for its next mission.)

Practice Guitar Regularly!

Now what can we learn from this insight into how your brain learns to play guitar? Something important, something vital! Since you are using your practice time to create and deepen a sequence of firing synapses, you'd better make sure that the sequence is correct! Otherwise you may end up with several ingrained sequences for your D chord. One of them will be the correct one, and the others will be WRONG. Perhaps you'll put your third finger down on the third string instead of the second string, or maybe you'll make an E chord instead.

The outcome is, according to the researchers, a simple matter of statistics. Let's say that half the time you practice your D chord correctly...a quarter of the time you practice your D chord with the third finger on the wrong string...and the rest of the time you accidentally make an extremely exotic chord, the D-major/minor7th chord. Then, after a month of practice, when you are in the middle of playing a song, you'll get this conversation between you and your brain:

You: "Gimme a D!"

Your Brain: BAM! (50 % of the time has made a D chord)

BAM! (25% of the time has made an incorrectly-fingered D chord)

BAM! (25% of the time has fingered a, D-major/minor7th chord)

The important thing to remember here is that at this point it is too late. Your conscious mind has little control over which D you'll get in the middle of a fast song.

What you practiced is what you got! That's why it is vital that you take the time at the beginning to create an accurate pattern in your mind.

Once you have gradually created the accurate pathway in your mind, you can then go through it quickly, and more quickly, and more quickly again. This idea is expressed by the Latin phrase "Festina Lente," or "Hurry Slowly." If you want to be a fast guitar player then don't worry about being a fast guitar player. Instead, make sure that you are an accurate guitar player, and you will also end up being a fast guitar player. When you want a D, you'll get a D, and when you want a D quickly, you'll get a D quickly.

To practice guitar accurately, remember this:

Festina Lente.
When you practice guitar, practice accurately to create accurate patterns in your mind and body.

If Something is Worth Doing, it is Worth Doing Well. Practice with Focus.

2. Practice Regularly.

We all have complicated lives. A thousand concerns push and pull us, a hundred desires and duties ask us for our limited time. It can be difficult to find the time or make the time to do even that which we most desire to do–such as practicing guitar. Yet we know that without practicing guitar, we cannot play guitar.

And there is a most effective way for this practice to occur–often! If a person can practice guitar several times over the course of a week, even for a shorter period of time, they will learn more than a person who practices only once in that week, even for a longer period of time. Each time you return to your instrument, it will be with a deeper understanding and a greater ability.

Make a regular time for your guitar practice. Don't go overboard: Set yourself a time and a place that make sense in your life. Some students practice first thing when they get home from work or school. Others practice after dinner. Think of a time and place that will work for you and make a commitment to practice several times a week at least. There may be a time when you don't feel motivated. Don't wait for motivation to strike, but start practicing and the motivation will follow. Of course, if you find yourself playing guitar for hours on end at all times of day and night, that also is OK.

If possible, leave your guitar out of its case on a guitar stand or leaning up against the wall so that it is especially easy to pick up and play. Its purpose is to be played, not to sit in a case!

By making the practice of an art a regular part of your life, you are becoming a practitioner of that art. Be a **practitioner** of guitar. Remember the words of Henry Wadsworth Longfellow:

The heights by great men
reached and kept,
Were not attained by sudden flight.
But they, while their
companions slept,
Were toiling upwards in the night.

3. Practice Effectively.

The guitar teacher and author David Mead tells a story about a famous classical musician. As a young British man in the 1940s, he was inducted into the National Service. He thought for sure that his music career was ended. But he thought "at least I can try to keep from losing ALL my musical skill and technique." So he made a plan to practice what he considered to be the very most vital elements of music for the short time each day he might get to keep for himself, just to try to stay even.

As the end of his service approached, he found to his surprise that he was a better musician than ever. Those few focused minutes per day were accomplishing more for his technique than hours of practice and playing had done before his enlistment. Why? The answer is this—FOCUS. He spent his limited time doing the very most important things in an intense, focused manner.

Let us do the same. When you sit down to practice, turn the TV off. Turn the radio off. Make a plan about what you will practice. And then pay attention to what you are doing! This focus will result in each practice session being as helpful, valuable and fulfilling as possible. As you practice with focus, you will feel great satisfaction in your inexorable progress as a guitarist.

At first, at the beginning of your practice sessions, you may find it difficult to focus. This is normal. Professor Mihaly Csikszentmihaly of the University of Chicago, has dedicated his life to the study of "flow," which is the state of complete immersion in an activity. He found in his research that to achieve this complete focus requires an initial effort, perhaps of 15 minutes. For this reason, it is best that you make your practice sessions at least 30 minutes long; for the first half of the session you may find yourself struggling to fully pay attention, and then you may be surprised by how quickly the second half flows by.

As you continue practicing guitar, you will find that it becomes easier and easier to enter this state of complete attention. Merely picking up your guitar and holding it in your lap and hands may become a trigger for relaxed focus.

Remember that old saying ***"if something is worth doing, it is worth doing well."*** It is worthwhile to play guitar, and it is worthwhile to play it well. Playing well does not mean performing incredible feats of musicianship—it means to play to the best of your ever-expanding ability, and to pay attention to what you are doing.

Fundamental Habits of a Good Guitar Player

Use your fingertip to fret notes, almost, but not quite, on the fret!

Use the very tip of your finger to fret a note; place the fingertip as close to the fret as you can without actually being on the fret.

Strum efficiently, using rest strokes.

Let your thumb rest against the thickest string of a chord; then let your hand drop and brush against the strings, coming to a rest against the guitar.

When changing chords, move the most important finger first!

For the G move the 2nd finger first; for the D move the 1st finger first.

Always play the optimum number of strings in a chord!

For G strum six strings and for D strum four strings.

Remember that the most important habit of a good guitar player is to practice!

Practice Suggestions for Class One

You will be doing yourself a service by becoming confident and comfortable with rest strokes and with your first two chords. You don't need to be fast—aim for CONFIDENCE and COMFORT. Practice at least three times for a half hour each. If you practice more, that would be great!

- ✓ **Warm up by making a D chord and playing the strings one by one, using rest strokes and striving for clarity on each string. Repeat with the G chord. Remember to play the correct number of strings on each chord—four on the D and six on the G.**
- ✓ **Change between D and G over and over and over, strumming each one in turn. Don't worry about speed or rhythm, but do remember to move the most important finger first (the 1st finger on D, and the 2nd finger on G).**
- ✓ **Play and sing your songs. Even if you do not consider yourself to be a great vocalist, singing with the songs will greatly improve your guitar playing.**
- ✓ **Mess around on the guitar. Fret different notes with different fingers; experiment.**

Do Yourself a Giant Favor, and Get an Electronic Tuner Now

My first guitar teacher said, "Dan, I've been playing guitar for 14 years and seven of those years have been spent tuning."

Please, I beg you, don't waste seven years of YOUR life. Do the second-most-useful thing* you can do to ensure your success as a guitar player—GET A TUNER!

When I got married, my wife and I were given two gift certificates by two different friends. One was a $150 gift certificate to a cookware store. The other one was a $150 gift certificate to a music store. I don't know what Miriam did with the first gift certificate, but I ran up to 48th Street (also known as "The Street of 1000 Guitar Shops") and spent the entire $150 on one single state-of-the-art tuner. Now, 10 years later, you can get an even better tuner for around $20, or even less! Where?

You can get a great electronic guitar tuner online from Musician's Friend or another on-line purveyor. You can download a tuning application for many phones.

You can also get a great electric tuner from Allan at Gotham Guitar Works (our neighbor here in the Recording and Rehearsal Arts Building), from 30th Street Guitars (across the street from our building, near the old Fire Station), any Guitar Center or Sam Ash, or virtually any music-related store.

Don't worry about how to use it—we'll cover that in the next lesson!!

* THE FIRST-MOST-USEFUL THING IS TO PRACTICE.

Dear NYC Guitar School Student—

I have written this little note to you from my heart.

You want to play guitar. In fact, you want to play guitar so much that you put your hard-earned money on the line and signed up for a class at New York City Guitar School. I know you didn't do that lightly, and I don't take it for granted.

Even more importantly, you made a commitment of your time. As a busy person in New York City, I know how precious your time is. It is difficult to balance work and responsibilities, and still find the time to make your dreams come true.

I have good news for you. At New York City Guitar School, we have developed what I believe is the world's most effective curriculum for learning to play rock guitar. This curriculum has been created especially for the busy New York City adults who are our students. The lessons have been constantly rewritten and tested on over one thousand people who have successfully learned to play guitar.

Furthermore, we have dedicated and expert teachers who give their all to help their students be successful. We hire less than ten percent of those who seek a position here, and they are not allowed to teach this course until they have spent months teaching private lessons, becoming familiar with the curriculum, and proving their commitment to their students. I feel very fortunate to work with them!

But good as our curriculum is, it cannot guarantee that you will play guitar. And as gifted as your teacher may be, he or she cannot make you a guitar player, either. Only one person on this planet can ensure that you learn to play guitar.

That is YOU.

The students who have successfully learned to play guitar in this course practiced three times per week, for a half hour at a time. Some practiced more, but those who practiced three times each week made steady progress. They also attended class regularly. If they had to miss a class, they called the school at 646-485-7244 to schedule a make-up class or free mini-lesson.

Please take a moment right now to make a commitment to yourself to regular practice and attendance over the next ten weeks. In class ten, when you perform for your classmates, you will be astounded by how much you've learned, and how much fun you've had.

Congratulations on deciding to PLAY GUITAR!

Sincerely,

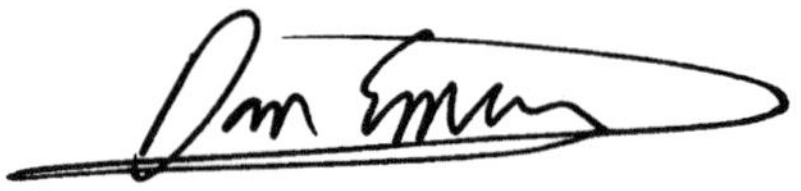

Dan Emery
Founder, New York City Guitar School

P.S. Please do not hesitate to call me at 646-485-7244 with any comment or concern!

P.P.S. If you must miss your class, please arrange to make it up by attending the same lesson on another day or night, or with a free mini-lesson. Mini-lessons are 15 minutes long, and are taught by super-patient and friendly teachers. Please call 646-485-7244 or drop by the office to reserve your time. All your classes must be made up within a week of the end of your course.

CLASS ONE SONGS
D to G

You know the D chord. You know the G chord. These are the most important two chords you'll ever learn, because they are your first chords. Every future chord will just be another chord.

Surprisingly, you can already play songs with only these two chords. I've listed some below, along with a little short-cut approximate chord progression applicable to each one. The way these little charts (which you'll see many of in your guitar career) work is that in each four-beat measure, there is a letter for the chord. For example:

① 2 3 4 ① 2 3 4
|: D | G :|

means "Play a D chord on the first beat of one measure, and play a G chord on the first beat of the other." The ":" means "repeat."

① 2 ③ 4
|: D G :|

on the other hand, means play "D on the first beat and G on the third beat of the measure."

Working from more beats between changes to fewer, **"Born in the USA" by Bruce Springsteen** is based on a progression like this one:

① 2 3 4 etc.
|: D | D | D | D |
| G | G | G | G :|

"Feel Like Making Love" by Bad Company, "Baby You Can Drive My Car" by The Beatles (verse), **"Take A Walk on The Wild Side" by Lou Reed, "You Sexy Thing" by Hot Chocolate** (capo III)* and **"Bells Ring" by Mazzy Star** (capo V) are based on the same change over two measures, along these lines:

① 2 3 4 etc.
|: D | G :|

And as you get faster, smoother and more confident with your D to G you can try something like **"What I Got" by Sublime,** which is based on the same change within just one measure:

① 2 ③ 4
|: D G :|

Here is my recommendation to you—first practice changing from D to G lots and lots and lots. Once you get comfortable, get a copy of "What I Got" and try to play along strumming each chord once. That's fast! Here's a practice progression for you to play:

Early

① 2 3 4 etc.
|: D | G | D | G |
| D | G | D | G :|

* YOU WILL LEARN ALL ABOUT CAPOS IN CLASS THREE.

CLASS ____ PRACTICE CHART: ______________________________

Your teacher will assign you something great to fill in on this page! (If you're studying this book on your own, then use this page as a worksheet to figure out and write down an entire song you'd like to practice, or just write your own if you prefer.)

RHYTHM: | 1 + 2 + 3 + 4 + |

PRACTICE TAB, LICK or RIFF

T
A
B

CLASS

2

The Single Most Important Habit of a Good Guitarist is Playing in Rhythm

~ by Dan Emery of NYC Guitar School ©2009 ~

{ *Using a tuner; playing with a pick; strumming on the beat—quarter-note strums; the A7 chord; how to practice; how to read tablature and play cool licks; memorize songs.* }

Good Guitarists Play in Tune

The first thing most guitarists do when they pick up a guitar is to TUNE it using an electronic tuner. I used to be a purist. "I learned how to tune by ear, and so should everybody," I'd say. Then I realized that students who used tuners progressed faster than other students, and even learned to tune by ear better, because they knew what "in-tune" sounded like. Now I think that a tuner is the single most important tool a guitarist can have. As I mentioned last week, mine cost $150, but technology has advanced so rapidly you can get a better one for $10-$20.

To use a tuner, we need to know the names of the strings. A useful mnemonic device is "Elephants And Deers Got Big Ears." This grammatically incorrect statement is true; elephants and deer do have big ears, and the names of the strings from thick to thin are E-A-D-G-B-E. Remember—The thickest string is the "Elephant" string, also called the "low E" string because it is the lowest, deepest-sounding string. The thinnest string, the "Ears" string, is called the "high E" string because it is the highest, brightest-sounding string. See below for several helpful sketches of strings and tuners.

Let's tune! There are two types of tuners, manual and chromatic. Turn yours on. If you have a manual tuner, switch it to the "E/6" setting. Put the tuner on your leg right next to the guitar, and boldly play the sixth string with a rest stroke.

If the note is perfectly in tune, the arrow, pointer, light or other display element will be centered. If the note is too low-pitched, the arrow, etc. will point to the left of center. If the note is too high-pitched, the

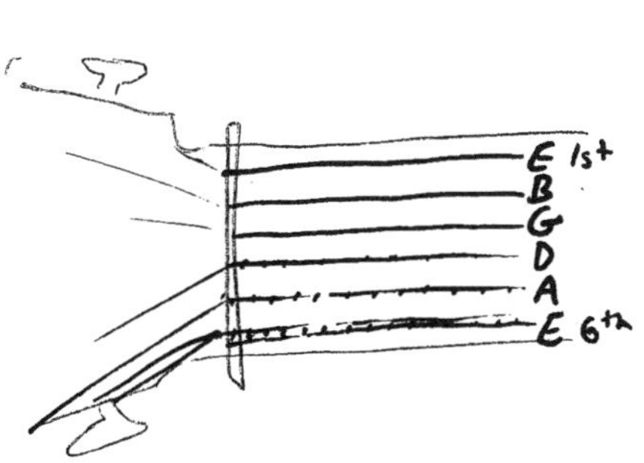

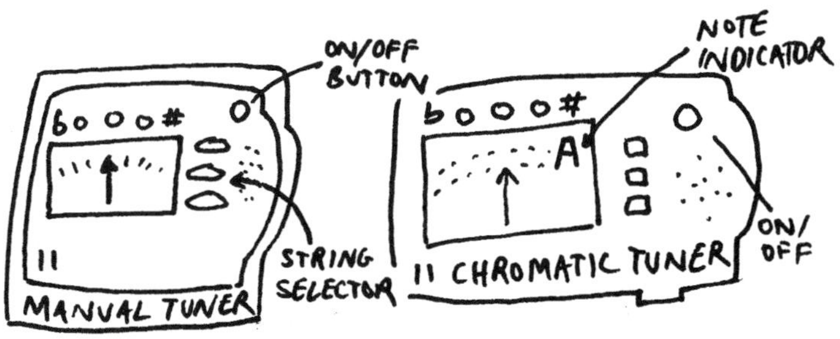

arrow, etc. will point to the right of center. In either case, reach out with your fretting hand, grab the tuner at the end of the sixth string, and turn it. By experimenting you'll soon discover which direction tightens the string, making it higher pitched, and which loosens the string, making it lower pitched. Every so often strum the string again until the display is centered.

Now those of you with chromatic tuners, congratulations! Your chromatic tuner is the bee's knees, and can be used for many arcane tuning needs which you may or may not ever need. Still, there is an extra step. FIRST you must approximately tune the guitar. When you play that E string, ignore the pointer and instead look for the note display, which will tell you what note the string is currently approximately making. If the display says D or E♭ ("♭" is pronounced "flat" and means "a half step lower than") or another note lower than E, then you need to tighten the string until the note display says E. If the display says F, G♭, F♯ ("♯" is pronounced "sharp" and means "a half step higher than") or another note higher than E then you need to loosen the string until the note display says E. Once the note display says E, continue tuning using the centering display.

The Pick

Section 2.3.1. To Pick or Not to Pick

Many great players use only thumbs and fingers to pluck and strum. Most country, rock, folk, pop and punk guitarists use picks. Those who play nylon string (classical) guitars prefer fingers. Fingers are well suited for fingerpicking. Most steel-string players use picks, which rarely blister.

Section 2.3.2. Descriptions

Called pick, plectrum, flat pick. Made of plastic, nylon, tortoiseshell, steel, even felt. Usually teardrop or triangle shaped. Sizes include too big, too small and just right. Thicknesses include really thick, kinda thick, not so thick, thinner than tracing paper. Billy Gibbons of ZZ Top cut up his credit cards and used them as picks.

Section 2.3.3. Holding the Pick

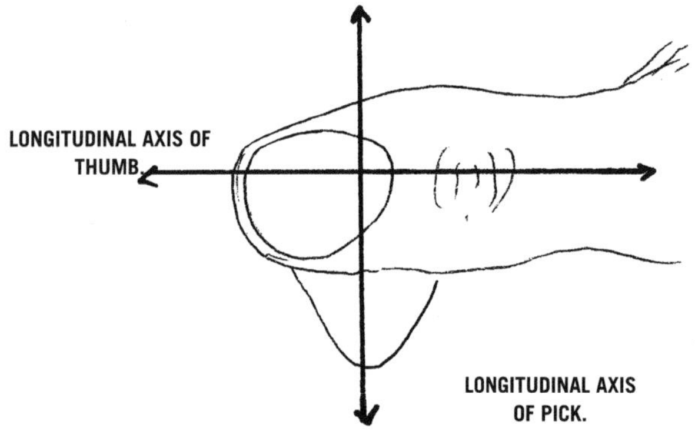

Fig. A. Relationship of pick to thumb.

Fig. B. The crease of the first joint of the first finger is a handy place to tuck a pick.

Section 2.3.4. Using the Pick

Step One: Line up pick with thumb. (See Fig. A.)

Step Two: Use index finger to hold pick against thumb. Do not hold too firmly. Do not hold too loosely. Experiment.

Step Three: Strum.

Step 2.3.5. Additional Details

At first holding, a pick may seem awkward, especially when you drop it into the sound hole of your guitar.

The Most Important Element of Guitar Greatness

So far you've been working the PHYSICAL side of playing guitar. You haven't been making much music—you've been teaching your hands to make a D and a G chord, and you've been internalizing important habits through exercise. These habits include:

- Strumming the correct number of strings in a chord with a beautiful, efficient rest stroke.
- Using the fingertips to fret the strings very close to the fret.
- When changing chords, planting the most important finger first (D=1st, G=2nd)

Good job! Your D and G chords give you HARMONY—nice-sounding combinations of notes. But to make music we need more than just harmony. We need RHYTHM! So grab your guitar and read on, because you are about to learn the single most essential skill of a good guitarist—playing in rhythm!

That's right, being "on the beat" is more important than making a nice-sounding chord. Let's perform a thought experiment. Imagine that you're sitting around a campfire with friends, strumming your guitar in perfect rhythm, and everybody's singing along, when suddenly you go to a G chord but finger it quite badly. It's more like an X chord—but you keep strumming anyway as though it was a perfect chord.

What happens? Most of your friends don't even notice, that's what! They just keep on drunkenly singing! And afterwards, they refer to you behind your back as "an amazing guitar player." Why? Because you were IN RHYTHM—Job One of any guitarist.

Let's imagine a different scenario. There you are playing next to the campfire, your friends are singing along, you move to that pesky G chord and realize that you can't make the change in time. So you **wait to strum** until you've formed the perfect chord, and only then do you strum. What happens now? **Disaster**—everybody gets off rhythm, the song comes crashing to a halt, somebody starts telling a ghost story, and your so-called friends hide your guitar behind some rocks.

From this simple parable, we learn that THE MOST IMPORTANT JOB OF A GUITARIST IS TO PLAY IN RHYTHM! Of course, we want "good chord, good rhythm"—but we also want to know what our priority is. It is rhythm. Let's talk about it.

About 95% of the songs you hear are "in 4," or played with a feeling of four beats. Songs in a feeling of four are usually said to be in 4/4 time, which for right now we can think of as meaning 4 beats at a time, over and over. To get an idea of what I am talking about, you're going to tap your foot slowly and evenly, and with each tap of your foot, say a number. This is very important, and we need to be able to do it to play ACTUAL SONGS. Your foot will never speed up or slow down—your voice will be even. Got it? Good, now start slowly and evenly tapping your foot, and then begin speaking along:

ONE two three four ONE two three four ONE two three four ONE two three four (etc.)

Do this until you are comfortable and confident with counting and tapping your foot. Remember, no beat is ever faster or slower than any other beat—keep the timing of each beat absolutely even.

Strumming in Rhythm

Now that you know how to tap and count, let's get the guitar involved. You're going to make a G chord. You're going to get your right hand ready to strum. You're going to begin tapping your foot slowly and evenly, just as before. You're going to begin counting along slowly and evenly, just as before. But THIS time, in addition to tapping and counting, you will also calmly strum down across all six strings each time that you say a number. This is called "playing on the beat"—and if you can learn to do this, you are destined for success.

So make a G chord, start tapping, start counting aloud and start strumming along with every one, two, three and four. Do this several times. (I've written the numbers as numerals instead of words.)

The Most Important Job of a Good Guitarist is to STRUM ON THE BEAT!

① ② ③ ④ ① ② ③ ④ ① ② ③ ④ ① ② ③ ④

Measures and Bars

In this next set of "one-two-three-four's," I've divided each set of four beats with a vertical slash. In music, each of these sets of four is called a MEASURE of music. Among the cooler rocker types, a measure is often called a BAR of music. We are those cool rocker types, so we'll usually call those things bars. I'll also put a "D" over the top of each measure, to signify that you will be playing D chords.

So make a D chord, start tapping and counting, and strum on each beat in the following four bars. Do this several times.

D **D** **D** **D**

| ① ② ③ ④ | ① ② ③ ④ | ① ② ③ ④ | ① ② ③ ④ |

This Chapter's Big Fun: Changing Chords in Rhythm

You are just a few minutes away from changing chords in perfect rhythm! To do so, you'll not only need to play in rhythm as you've been doing, but to change chords at the same time. We'll use D and G. Why don't you prepare by practicing this change for a moment? Remember to lead with the first finger when changing to D and the second finger changing to G.

Got it? Good. At the end of this paragraph you'll start tapping, you'll start counting aloud, and you'll strum the D chord right on the "one." Then **as you continue to** count and tap your foot and strum on each beat, you'll move your fingers into the G chord, and strum IT right on the "one" and subsequent beats. Then you'll change back to D and strum, then to G again, and so on. Do this slowly and evenly and remember that **the strumming hand is most important!** KEEP IT MOVING EVENLY AND STEADILY, even while changing chords. This is called "locking your hand in with the beat."

D **G** **D** **G**

| ① ② ③ ④ | ① ② ③ ④ | ① ② ③ ④ | ① ② ③ ④ |

Lock Your Hand in With the Beat

This means moving your hand exactly with the beat—not rushing, but just confidently letting your hand fall into a strum exactly when each beat falls. It's the single most important skill in rock and roll. It is **much more** important to keep steadily strumming in an even tempo than it is to play a clean-sounding chord.

This is **vital!** If the change is a little too challenging, simply tap your foot more slowly. Spend some time with this exercise, building skill and confidence. Don't worry too much about how clear the chords sound or even if you are correctly strumming four strings on the D and six on the G. Although those things are important, let us take care of our first priority—strumming the chord right on the beat.

Take your time. Recall that ideally, you strum four strings on the D and six on the G—but also recall that a good guitarist always takes care of the most important thing first—and strumming on the beat is the most important thing. Spend five minutes, or 15 minutes, or 50 minutes on this exercise—when you feel confident and consistent, the time is right to move on. (Sometimes students find it helpful to break the chord change into one finger move per beat. On the D that would be the first finger, then the second, then the third. On the G that would be the second finger, then third, then the first.)

Strumming evenly on each beat is THE essential guitar skill. Even the most advanced rock-star guitarist is often strumming right on the beat exactly as you are doing.

The A7 Chord

Right now, you are the grand master of D and G. Sadly, there aren't very many songs you can play with only two chords—but with three chords you can play literally thousands. We need one more chord to put those songs in your reach, and here it is—the A7 chord. Don't worry right now about what the "7" means—just assume it is a lucky number for you. Here is the chord diagram for an A7 chord. (These things are used so often in guitar that soon you'll be reading them like a pro!)

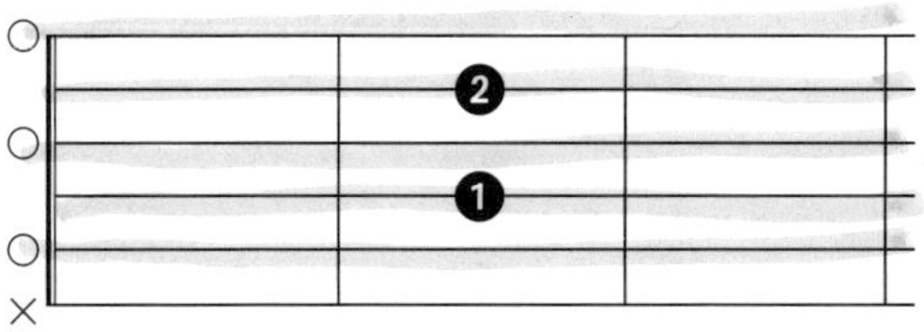

A7

In this chord, the first finger is your plant finger. Once again, become basically familiar with the chord—repeatedly finger the chord, leading with your first finger, and then strum five strings. Occasionally check to hear that each string rings out clearly, asking yourself these very important questions:

Am I using my fingertips to fret the chord?
Am I fretting close to (but not on top of) the frets?
Am I pushing the strings against the frets?

Change chords between the D and the A7. Don't worry about strumming on every beat at first. Just strum every time you say "one." To remind you to strum just on the one, I've circled each "1" below. Count, tap and play:

D | **A7** | **D** | **A7**
| ① 2 3 4 | ① 2 3 4 | ① 2 3 4 | ① 2 3 4 |

Now let's do this using the single most important skill of any guitarist—playing on every beat. Count slowly, strum evenly. To show you that we are strumming on every beat, I've circled every beat below.

D | **A7** | **D** | **A7**
| ①②③④ | ①②③④ | ①②③④ | ①②③④ |

Repeat these exercises with G and A7. Remember to lead with your second finger on the G and your first finger on the A7. Count and play:

G | **A7** | **G** | **A7**
| ① 2 3 4 | ① 2 3 4 | ① 2 3 4 | ① 2 3 4 |

And then:

G | **A7** | **G** | **A7**
| ①②③④ | ①②③④ | ①②③④ | ①②③④ |

How to Read Tablature and Use it to Play Cool Licks

YOU'VE BEEN PLAYING GUITAR for perhaps a week right now, and I'm sure you are constantly wondering "Why can't I play cool licks yet, such as 'Stairway to Heaven,' or the guitar theme to the old TV show 'Batman,' or the lead guitar part from 'Smells Like Teen Spirit' by Nirvana?"

Q: *Dan, what is a lick?*
A: A "lick" is a neat little guitar part, usually made up of single notes. It is called a "lick" because it sounds so tasty.

Now is the time for you to learn the awesome power of tablature and to begin playing lead guitar. Tablature is a system of writing music for the guitar that was developed by flamenco guitarists in 15th-century Spain.

Here is how it works. Do you remember our trusty chord diagram?

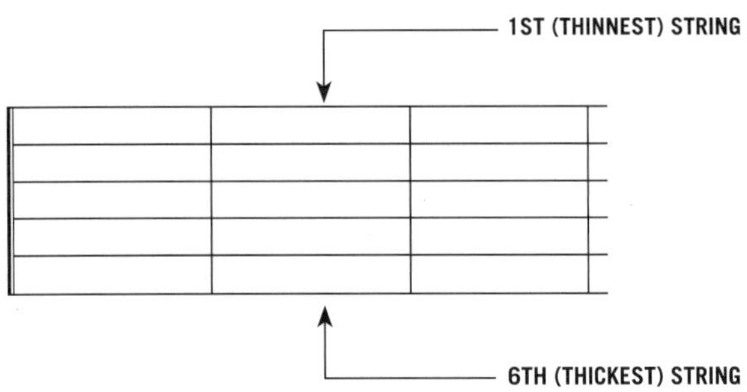

Tablature is based on the same idea; there are six lines, each corresponding to one of the six strings on the guitar. The line at the top stands for the first and thinnest string. The line at the bottom stands for the sixth and thickest string. Just as in a chord diagram, the lines depict an aerial view of the guitar strings, or a tracing of the guitar strings with the head at the left where it says "TAB"

Now to tell you what to play, the person writing tablature will write a number over one of the lines. This number will tell you two things—first, that you should play the indicated string; second, that you should play it at the indicated fret. Read and play through the following examples:

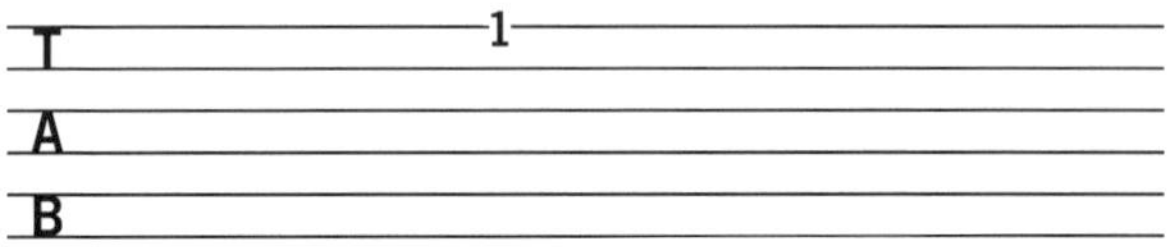

MEANS "PLAY THE FIRST STRING AT THE FIRST FRET"

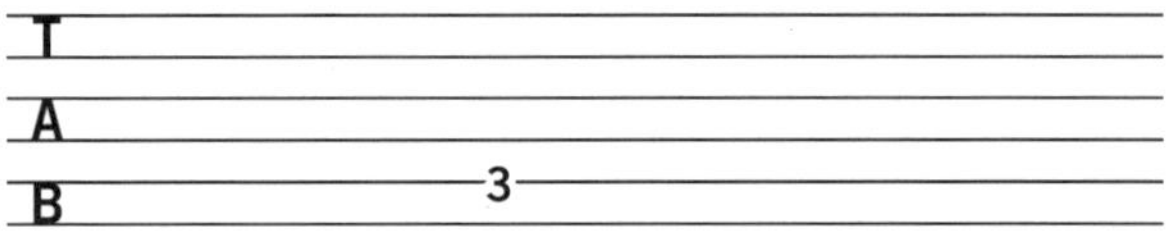

MEANS "PLAY THE FIFTH STRING AT THE THIRD FRET"

When you're supposed to play the string open, without fretting it, the writer will place a zero on the string/line in question. For example:

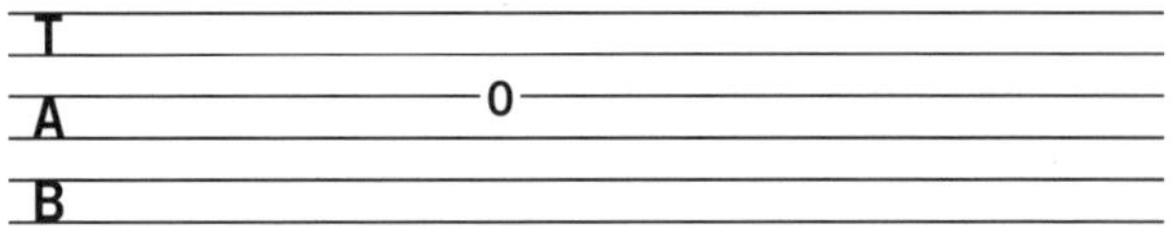

MEANS "PLAY THE THIRD STRING OPEN"

By the way, let's notice something important that tablature doesn't tell us—it **doesn't** say what finger to use! Never think that the numbers in a tab have anything to do with what finger you're supposed to use.

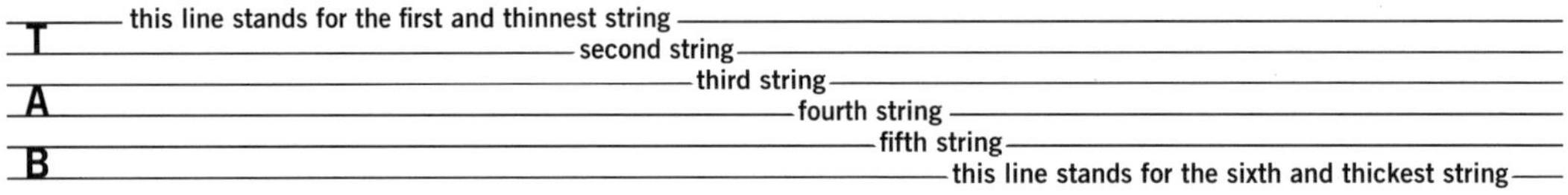

Sometimes more than one string is played at the same time. This is shown by stacking the notes on top of each other. For example:

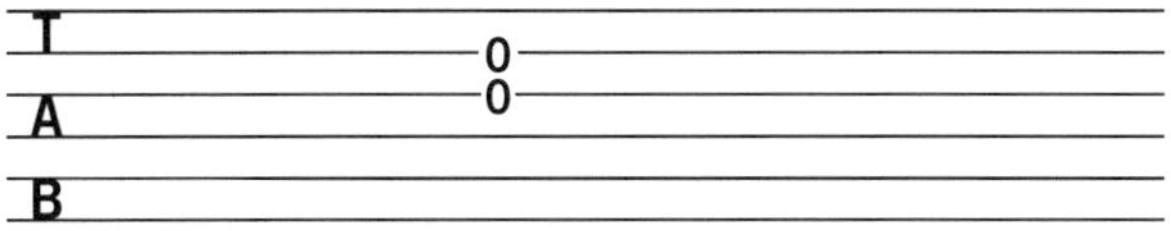

MEANS "PLAY THE THIRD AND THE SECOND STRING OPEN AT THE SAME TIME"

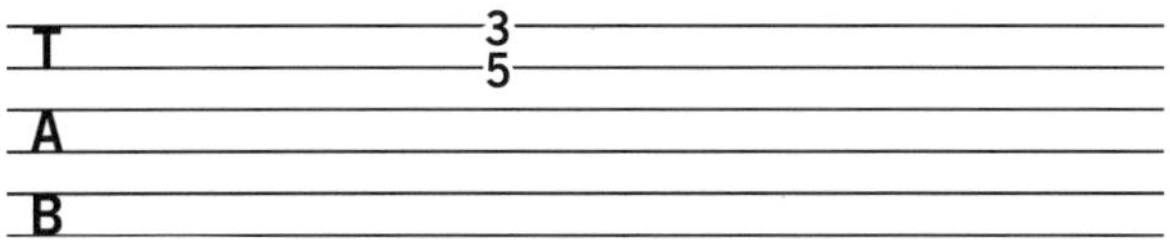

MEANS "PLAY THE FIRST STRING AT THE THIRD FRET AND SECOND STRING AT THE FIFTH FRET AT THE SAME TIME"

Often a complicated-looking tab notation is just telling you to play an open chord! For example:

MEANS "PLAY THE D CHORD!"

Tablature shows the time element of music by moving left to right–in other words, you first play whatever is written on the left, then you play the next note, then the next and so on.

MEANS "PLAY THE FIRST STRING OPEN, THEN AT THE FIRST FRET, THEN AT THE SECOND, THEN AT THE THIRD"

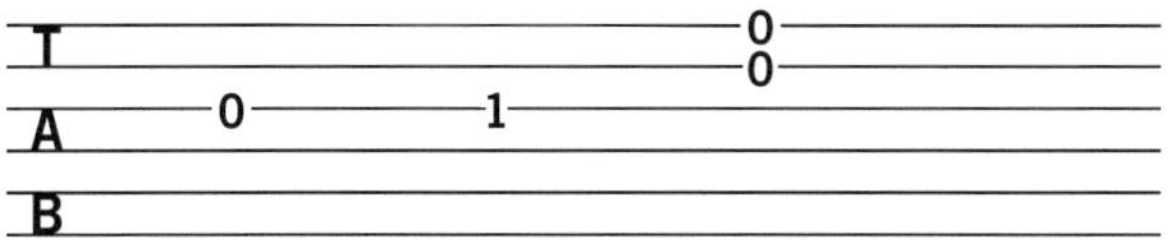

MEANS "PLAY THE THIRD STRING OPEN, THEN AT THE FIRST FRET, THEN PLAY THE FIRST AND SECOND STRINGS OPEN AT THE SAME TIME"

Again, sometimes a complicated-looking tablature is simply a chord written out. For example:

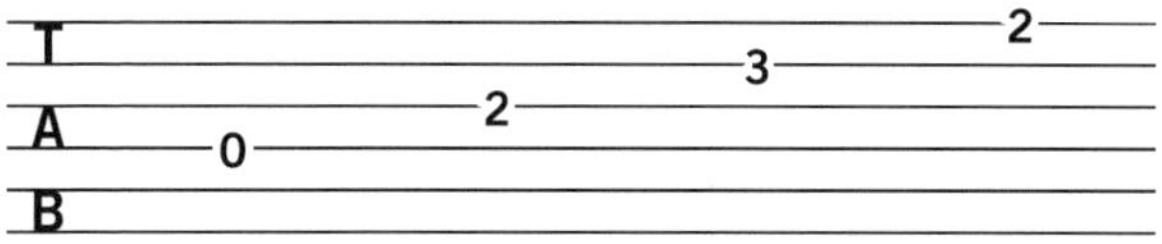

MEANS "PLAY THE D CHORD ONE STRING AT A TIME —FIRST THE OPEN FOURTH STRING, THEN THE FRETTED THIRD STRING, THEN THE FRETTED SECOND STRING, AND FINALLY THE FRETTED FIRST STRING"

If you can read and play through all the preceding examples, then you have a great beginning understanding of tablature: Now, it is true that there are lots of other symbols showing techniques such as the "scratch," "slide," "hammer-on," "bend," "vibrato" and so on. You'll gradually be introduced to them. But we won't worry about those right now.

Now you theoretically have the ability to play your favorite songs note for note.

"Note for note" means "exactly as the original artist played it." In many cases, the original artist would never play it exactly the same way twice. Real feeling and understanding are always more important than rote memorization. That said, it's a lot of fun to play something just the way your favorite guitarist did, and it's great for your technique!

Many of your favorite songs have been written out in tablature and are available in books sold at fine music stores, book stores and web sites. Furthermore, millions of amateur guitarists have attempted to figure out how to play their favorite songs and have posted their tabs on the Internet. Some of them are quite good. So if you want to play, say, a Coldplay song note for note, you can either purchase the official Coldplay book, which will contain an extremely accurate transcription, or you can search for "Coldplay guitar tab" on the Internet and have your choice of many different tabs of greater or lesser accuracy. Although things change quickly on the Internet, popular tab sites include ultimate-guitar.com and chordie.com.

Let me stress, though, that good guitar music is not written down on paper—it exists as sound and feeling—so regardless of which tab you might use to figure out how to play your favorite song, it is **vital** and **essential** that you have a copy of the original song to listen to and play along with! So really **listen to** your Coldplay CD, or your AFI CD, or your, uh, AC/DC CD, before, during and after learning to play a lick or song note for note.

> **Good Guitarists Memorize Songs by Perceiving Patterns in Music!**
>
> Usually these patterns are in sets of four!

Your First Cool Lick Written out in Tablature

Since tablature doesn't give the proper fingering, I've written the recommended left-hand finger below each note. Since tablature doesn't give pick direction, I've written the recommended right-hand picking direction above each note (⊓ = down, ∨ = up). Since tablature doesn't give timing, I've also written the timing above each measure.

Cool Lick # 1

This lick is FANTASTIC for teaching your left and right hand to work together. It also is great for teaching your right hand to lock in with the beat, moving down on every beat and up in between beats. Also it is fun to play and fun to listen to. When playing this at a party, don't forget to occasionally yell "Batman!"

Remember your fundamental great habits of playing guitar: Use your fingertips close to the frets. Be efficient—don't let your left-hand fingers get too far away from the guitar. You want a nice, smooth transition between notes, rather than a staccato, pecking-chicken effect. Play slowly and evenly so that you can lock your hand in with the beat.

Practicing Licks

Licks should be practiced and mastered just like chord changes. Go slowly at first, and go correctly. Your fingers and mind are learning important skills as you practice these fancy moves. Gradually build your speed as your confidence and clarity improve.

Memorize Songs

Did you know that when a professional guitarist plays a five-minute song by heart, he or she has not memorized five minutes of music? That's right—experienced

Cool Lick # 1

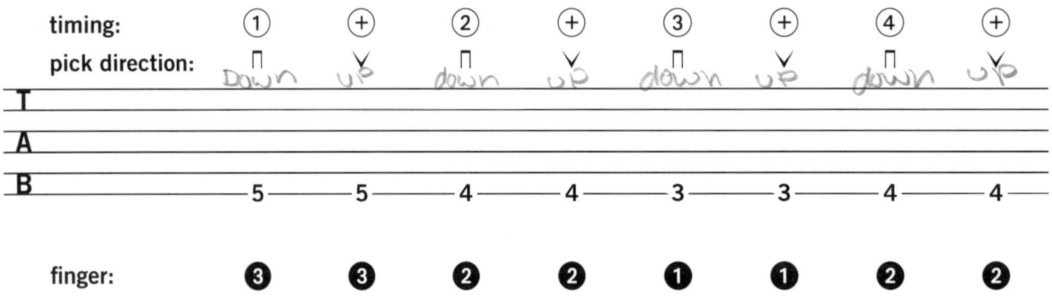

guitar players think of songs in terms of fairly short sections that repeat many times over the course of a song. A very typical arrangement of a song, for example, would be an eight-bar verse repeated several times over the course of a song, and a four-bar chorus that is also repeated several times.

Do you think you could memorize the following progression? (A "progression" is a series of chords.)

D D D D G G D D

Of course you could! Now, do you think you can memorize this next progression?

A7 G D D

Take a moment to commit each of those chord progressions to memory. Congratulations! You've learned a great song by heart! Get used to memorizing sets of four and eight chords, because nearly every progression in guitar music is either four bars, or a multiple of four bars, long.

Class Review

1. Good Guitarists Play on the Beat: Rhythm is Most Important!

When playing, keep the strumming hand moving in perfect rhythm. This is more important than good fretting, clean changes and accurate strumming. In guitar, as in life, do what is most important, and in guitar that is locking your hand in with the beat!

2. Good Guitarists Play Songs by Heart.

To memorize songs, look for and recognize patterns in the music, especially sets of four and eight.

Practice Suggestions for Class Two

Practice at least three times for half-an-hour each! If you practice more, that would be great!

- ✓ **Warm up by reviewing tablature and playing Cool Lick # 1 incessantly. Take your time—you are not yet striving for speed, but you do want to grow in confidence, clarity and comfort.**
- ✓ **Make each of your three chords and strum string by string for clarity.**
- ✓ **Play and sing your songs. Memorize them, words and music alike.**
- ✓ **Incessantly change chords, when you listen to music or watch TV, leading with the most important finger.**

Review of Previous Habits

Use your fingertip to fret notes, almost, but not quite, on the fret!

Use the very tip of your finger to fret a note; place the fingertip as close to the fret as you can without actually being on the fret.

Strum efficiently, using rest strokes.

Let your thumb rest against the thickest string of a chord; then let your hand drop and brush against the strings, coming to a rest against the guitar.

When changing chords, move the most important finger first!

For the G move the 2nd finger first; for the D move the 1st finger first.

Always play the optimum number of strings in a chord!

For G strum six strings and for D strum four strings.

Remember that the most important habit of a good guitar player is to practice!

CLASS TWO SONGS
D, G, A7

THE 12-MEASURE PROGRESSION below is an extremely common music structure called the 12-bar blues. You can use these to play **The Beatles' "Why Don't We Do It in the Road"** (capo VII), **Chuck Berry's "Johnny B. Goode"** (capo VIII), **Jimi Hendrix's "Red House"** (capo VIII), **Van Halen's "Ice Cream Man"** (capo I) and many others.

① ② ③ ④ etc.

: D	D	D	D
G	G	D	D
A7	G	D	D :

Sometimes songs follow the 12-bar blues with a little twist. For example, "Wipe Out" is a 12-bar blues without chord strums—instead, for most of the song, a single note lead guitar line follows the (implied) chord changes. **"I Still Haven't Found What I'm Looking For" by U2** follows a 12-bar blues pattern, except that the first eight bars are repeated before going onto the final four bars.

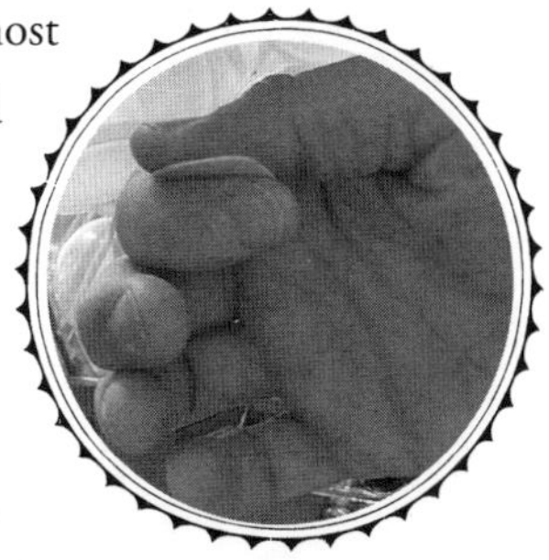

PICK
Here's an example of a well held pick.

I'm calling the following practice progression "Where Is My Guitar Pick?" in honor of that U2 song and also because, right at the moment I cannot find my guitar pick. To adapt this progression to play **"I Still Haven't Found What I'm Looking For,"** as always, get a copy of the song and listen to it, then try to play along.

Where is My Guitar Pick?

Verse

① ② ③ ④ etc.

|: D | D | D | D |
| G | G | D | D :|

Chorus

|: A7 | G | D | D :|

CLASS ____ PRACTICE CHART: ____________________

Your teacher will assign you something great to fill in on this page! (If you're studying this book on your own, then use this page as a worksheet to figure out and write down an entire song you'd like to practice, or just write your own if you prefer.)

RHYTHM: | 1 + 2 + 3 + 4 + |

PRACTICE TAB, LICK or RIFF

T
A
B

CLASS

3

Learn This and Learn Many of the Greatest Songs of All Time

~ by Dan Emery of NYC Guitar School ©2009 ~

{ *Pivot changes and how and why to use them; E minor, C major and D7; the concept of progressions; song sections to practice pivot changes.* }

Q: WHAT DO THESE SONGS ALL HAVE IN COMMON? "Stay Just A Little Bit Longer" by Jackson Browne, "Love Hurts" by Nazareth, "Every Breath You Take" by The Police, "Crocodile Rock" by Elton John, "Oh Donna" by Richie Valens, "Last Kiss" by Pearl Jam, "Dream" by The Everly Brothers," "Blue Moon" by Elvis, "Stand By Me" by Ben King, "Joey" by Concrete Blond, "Crazy" by Aerosmith, "Complicated" by Avril Lavigne, "The Reason" by Hoobastank AND MORE!

A: They are all based, in some fashion, on a single AMAZINGLY POWERFUL chord progression. This happens all the time in music; melodies and lyrics change, but the chords remain the same. A "chord progression" usually refers to a repeating series of chords, and this one goes like this:

G Em C D (or D7)

While we learn this progression, we're also going to learn one of the fundamental habits of a good guitar player—pivoting—which means leaving your fingers down whenever possible. A good guitar player is efficient.

Begin learning to pivot and play all these great songs by making your G chord. As always, remember to use your fingertips and play close to the frets.

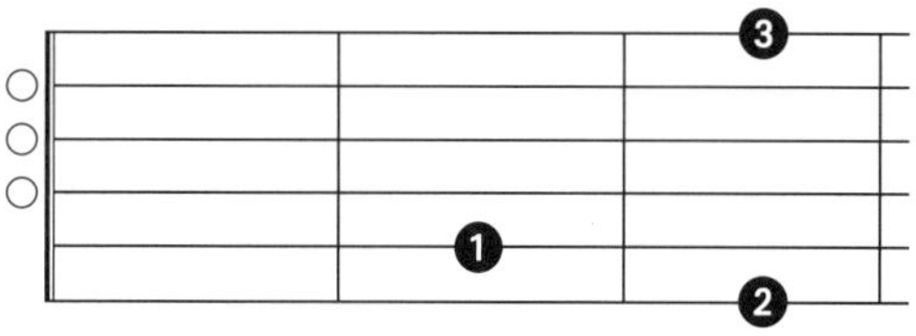

G

The E minor chord

Now, pivot to an E minor chord by LEAVING YOUR FIRST FINGER DOWN. End up in:

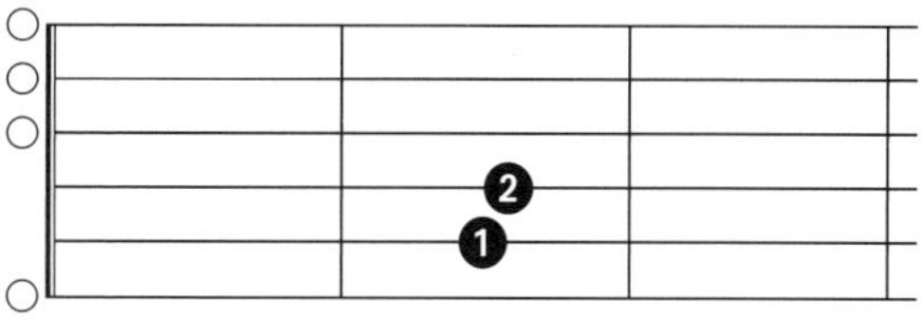

Em

Minor chords are usually described as sad-sounding chords. "Comfortably Numb" by Pink Floyd, "Heart of Gold" by Neil Young, and "Losing My Religion" by R.E.M. are examples of songs which begin with a minor chord. Change back and forth between G and Em until you are comfortable with the change, strumming six strings on each chord, on the first beat. Then, build up to playing on EVERY beat. Remember that good guitarists lock their hands in with the beat. Keep your hand moving even when you are changing chords!

① + ② + ③ + ④ + ① + ② + ③ + ④ +

𝄆 G | Em 𝄇

The C major chord

The C major chord may be a stretch at first—soon it will be one of your favorites. Begin by putting your fingers down in an E minor. LEAVE YOUR SECOND FINGER DOWN—it's your PIVOT. Reach out with your third finger, then with your first, to form the C.

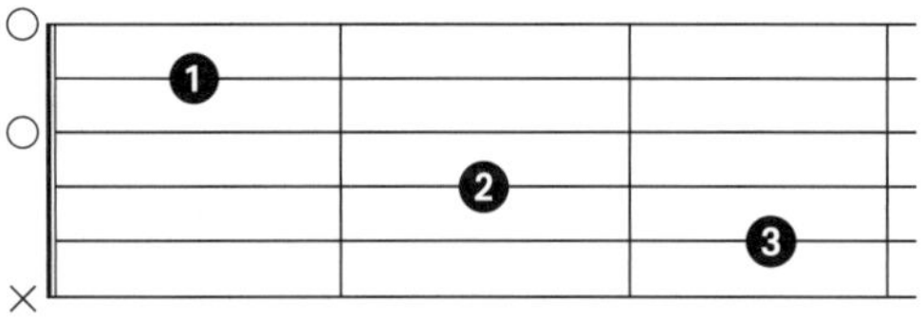

C

Then go back and forth between C and Em, pivoting with the second finger. Practice until you feel reasonably confident with this change, playing six strings on the E minor and five on the C major.

① + ② + ③ + ④ + ① + ② + ③ + ④ +

𝄆 Em | C 𝄇

The D7 chord

A seventh chord creates a feeling of motion—the need to travel to some other chord. The D7 chord, for example, is resolved by a move to a G chord. To learn the D7 chord, begin with a C chord. LEAVE THE FIRST FINGER DOWN—it's your PIVOT. Move your second finger and third finger to make the D7 chord, like so:

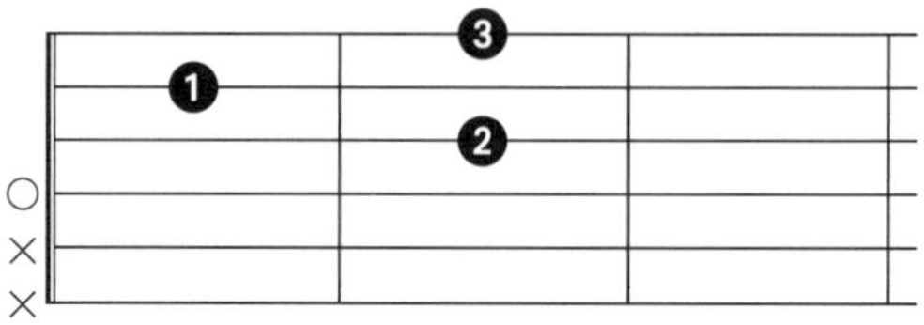

D7

Now make lots of exchanges between D7 and C. Play five strings on C, and four on D7. When you return to C from D7, really reach out with that third finger!

① + ② + ③ + ④ + ① + ② + ③ + ④ +

𝄆 C | D7 𝄇

The Whole Shebang

Now let's do the entire progression. Make a G and strum six strings. Then PIVOT with the first finger into the Em chord and strum six strings. Then PIVOT with the second finger into a C chord and play 5 strings. Finally, PIVOT with the first finger into a D7 chord and play 4 strings. Then return to a G chord by reaching out with your second finger. That's your plant. Now you're ready to begin again!

The Whole Shebang

① + ② + ③ + ④ + ① + ② + ③ + ④ +

𝄆 G | Em |

① + ② + ③ + ④ + ① + ② + ③ + ④ +

| C | D7 𝄇

An Important Note about Chord Progressions Which MUST be Understood to Get the Most from this Class!

Sometimes a student will learn that they can play a dozen or a thousand songs with the same few chords in the same order, and they will feel a little disappointed. "Oh," they'll say, "there's a trick to this—these songwriters aren't as creative as I thought—they all wrote a song using the same chords."

Q: *Did Picasso use the color blue? Did Picasso, the guy often called the greatest painter of all time, use the color blue? Did he?*
A: Yes, Dan—Picasso, the great painter, did use the color blue.

Q: *But didn't Van Gogh use the color blue, too? Didn't Georgia O' Keeffe use the color blue? Didn't Leonardo da Vinci use the color blue? Are these painters all copycat hacks, copying the color blue off of each other?*
A: They didn't use the color blue because they are copycat hacks. They were all great genius painters, and when you're a painter you use paint, and sometimes paint is blue. It's HOW you paint that makes you a great painter.

Similarly, when you're a songwriter, you use chord progressions. Thousands of songs have been written with the progression "G-Em-C-D", thousands more have been written with the twelve bar "A-A-A-A-D-D-A-A-E-D-A-E", hundreds more have been based on simply "C-F" and so on. The progression isn't what makes a song great—it's the EXPRESSION, the strums, rhythms, tone, technique, attitude, etc. that make a song great.

As a guitar player, you should be attuned to progressions. Usually they will come along in sets of four or eight measures. Constantly be on the lookout for patterns! Now, this doesn't always work, but after many glorious years spent figuring out how to play songs by listening to CDs and the radio, let me assure you that 99 percent of the songs you want to play contain solid repeating patterns. The more you attune to these patterns, the easier it is going to be for you to understand songs as the songwriter does, and to play songs by heart. So let's always look for patterns in chord progressions.

To Play *with* Heart, Play *by* Heart, by Noticing and Remembering Patterns in Music!

Now, it is a dream of mine for this guitar manual to someday be sitting on a shelf in the bookstore, filled with your favorite songs, note-for-note guitar parts, and exact lyrics. We haven't yet gotten the requisite permissions, so in the meantime, we must make a virtue of necessity. In each class, rather than learning an exact song, you'll learn a chord progression and strumming pattern which can be used to play **many** songs.

Sometimes you will find that it is quite easy to adapt this knowledge to play a particular song. For example, I will tell you that many songs are based on a D to G chord change, including "What I Got" by Sublime. Once you get comfortable with those chords, you will find it a very easy matter to listen to the song, and begin playing along. At other times the song won't be as obvious. In that case, follow these easy steps:

1. Most importantly, get the song and LISTEN to it. Then try to play along. Often, this will be enough.
2. If you still need help, you may need to get a chart. One way to do this is to search the internet for "guitar," "chart" and the name of the song and artist you're looking for.
3. Remember, practice makes perfect. Each time you adapt a basic progression to a particular song you will find it easier.

By the way, here at New York City Guitar School we often get calls from people who have played for years, but don't feel as confident as they think they ought to be. Why? Because they don't know any songs, that's why! Imagine—you begin playing guitar because you love songs, and you love the way the guitar sounds in those songs. You learn how to play 10 or 15 chords, and to strum through charts with different rhythms. After a couple of years of this, you walk into a room with a guitar resting in the corner, and you tell the guitar owner, "Hey, I play guitar, too!" "Wow!" exclaims the guitar owner (who is stunningly attractive), "will you play something for me?" And then you say, "Well, actually I don't remember how to play anything." Is that what you wanted when you set out to play guitar? Of course not!

This happens to people who never learn to look for and remember the patterns that are found in music. But it won't happen to you, because now and forever more you will remember songs by noticing the repeating four- and eight-measure patterns of which they consist!

Yes, picking out the patterns in music might be a little challenging in the beginning, just like learning a chord is a little challenging—but it is a learned skill and after a while it will become a habit for you. And when you play a song BY heart it is easier to play WITH your heart; it is easier to sing, to feel and to express yourself.

When a student asked the famous jazz guitarist Joe Pass what was the most important thing he could do to improve, he thought he'd be told to "practice scales" or "work on technique"—but Joe Pass told him to learn to play songs by heart, all the way through!

Capos and Their Care and Feeding

"Capo" means "head" in Italian. A Mafia capo is the head of a branch of a crime family. Please do not use a Mafia capo to help you play guitar. Instead, use a guitar capo, which is a device which squeezes all six of your guitar strings against whichever fret you place it behind, thus becoming the new "head" of the guitar. It is a tremendously useful tool, because it allows you to leverage just a few chords to be able to play along with lots and lots of different songs.

For example, this week you are learning the incredibly useful G to E minor to C to D7 progression, which can be used to play such songs as **"Stand By Me" by Ben King** and **"Stay Just A Little Longer" by Jackson Browne.** If you sing either of these songs while you play G to E minor to C to D7, you'll sound great! However, if you try playing along with the recordings, you will be in tune with Jackson Browne, but you will not be in tune with Ben King. Why? Because Ben King will not be playing G to E minor to C to D7. Instead, he will be playing A to F sharp minor to D to E—and you don't know these chords!

BUT, if you put your capo on the second fret, and then you play G to Em minor to C to D7, you will now be in tune with Ben King! You see, by putting the capo on the guitar, you changed the actual pitch of the notes you are holding down, so a G chord with a capo on the second fret is, strictly speaking, an A chord.

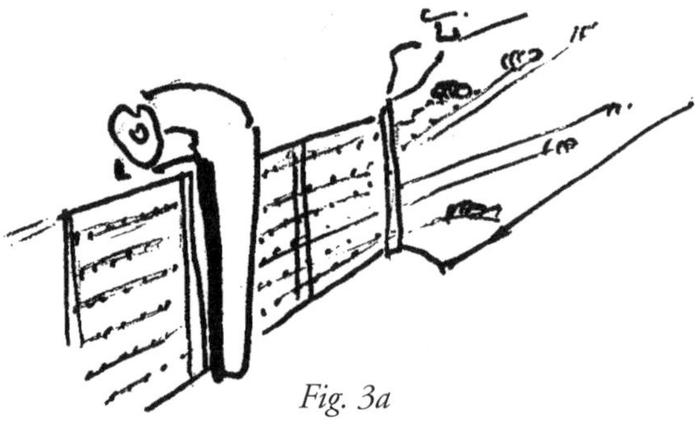

Fig. 3a

It is of **vital importance** that at this point you do not try to think of such a G chord as an A chord, though, because the whole point of a capo is to allow the guitarist to THINK in terms of the chords with which he or she is most familiar.

Figure 3a is a picture of a capo in action. Notice that the capo is placed near but not on the fret. This guitar is capoed at the second fret, ready to be played along with Ben King.

By the way, many long-haired, metal-head guitar-shredder types (i.e. me back in my Idaho woodshedding days) go through an "I don't need no stinking capo" phase. After a few years of playing guitar you might go through this phase, too, because you will know how to play an F sharp minor chord. But even such extremely experienced guitar players as Bob Dylan, Noel Gallagher of Oasis, Tom Petty and many, many more use capos routinely. So do I.

There are many types of capos, and just about any one of them will do the job. If you are at home right now reading this, and you do not have a capo handy, you can easily rig up a "poor man's capo" with a pencil and a couple of rubber bands!

Count and Play in 8th Notes as You Read Tab and Play a Cool Lick

As you know, there are typically four beats per measure of music. That is why when you strum "on the beat" you strum four times per bar. Just as a measure can be divided into four beats, so too a beat can be divided. If we divide it in half, we say that we are playing eighth notes, because we now have a total of eight notes per measure of four beats.

The note that happens exactly on the beat is counted as a "one" or a "two" or so on, and is said to be "on" the beat. A note that happens between the beats is counted as an "and" and is said to be "off" the beat.

Here is a great lick which is somewhat reminiscent of the guitar part from **Peter Gunn** and which will give all four of your fingers quite a workout. It will also help you to understand counting. Count aloud as you play the lick, and make sure that you play ON all the beats with a DOWN strum as you TAP your foot, and OFF the beats with an UP strum as you LIFT your foot!

Remember to count aloud when you first practice this lick! Understanding rhythm is important, and spending a week counting aloud as you tap your foot will be very helpful to your guitar career. Also remember your fundamental great habits of playing guitar; use your fingertips close to the frets. Be efficient—don't let your left hand fingers get too far away from the guitar. You want a nice, smooth transition between notes, rather than a staccato, pecking-chicken effect. Play slowly and evenly at first!

Somewhat But Not Quite Reminiscent of the Guitar Part from Peter Gunn

timing:	1	+	2	+	3	+	4	+
pick direction:	⊓	V	⊓	V	⊓	V	⊓	V
T								
A								
B	0	0	2	0	3	0	4	5
finger:	-	-	1	-	2	-	3	4

FUNDAMENTAL HABITS OF A GOOD GUITAR PLAYER

GOOD GUITARISTS KNOW THAT PLAYING IN RHYTHM IS MOST IMPORTANT!

GOOD GUITARISTS ARE EFFICIENT. LEAVE FINGERS DOWN WHENEVER POSSIBLE—PIVOT, PIVOT, PIVOT!

USE YOUR FINGERTIP TO FRET NOTES, ALMOST BUT NOT QUITE ON THE FRET.

STRUM EFFICIENTLY, USING REST STROKES.

WHEN CHANGING CHORDS, MOVE THE MOST IMPORTANT FINGER FIRST.

ALWAYS PLAY THE OPTIMUM NUMBER OF STRINGS IN A CHORD.

PERCEIVE AND REMEMBER PATTERNS IN MUSIC!

Practice Suggestions for Class Three

✓ Warm up by playing your cool lick from Class Three, incessantly, slowly and accurately.

✓ Pivot from G, to Em and back again over and over and over. Do the same thing with Em to C and with C to D7. You can sing and play your mini-songs. Every once in a while, strum your chords string by string to check for clarity.

G and Em: FIRST FINGER STAYS DOWN

Try singing "**About A Girl**" by **Nirvana** as you play this change.

① + ② + ③ + ④ + | ① + ② + ③ + ④ +

|: Em | G :|

Em and C: SECOND FINGER STAYS DOWN

Try singing the "**Ground Control to Major Tom**" **David Bowie** line with this change.

① + ② + ③ + ④ + | ① + ② + ③ + ④ +

|: C | Em :|

C and D7: FIRST FINGER STAYS DOWN

Try singing "**On Broadway**" by **Ben King** as you play these chords.

① + ② + ③ + ④ + | ① + ② + ③ + ④ +

|: D7 | C :|

✓ Play and sing all your songs, especially your G-Em-C-D7 song. Singing and playing songs all the way through is real guitar playing.

✓ Remember that studies show that it usually takes about 15 minutes to get into a practice session—so commit to practicing for a half-hour at a time, three times a week.

CLASS THREE SONGS
G, Em, C, D

THE E MINOR CHORD
The first finger is on the same string and same fret in both the Em and G chords, and can be left in place when changing between them.

THE G-EM-C-D7 CHORD progression is absolutely vital. It is the foundation for hundreds of songs. Playing one chord per measure gives you songs like **The 5 Satins' "In the Still of the Night,"** (capo very inconvenient, don't bother) and **"Last Kiss"** which was made most popular by **Pearl Jam** (open, meaning "no capo necessary"). Spend twice as long on each chord and you've got the basis for **"Joey" by Concrete Blond** (open) and **"The Reason" by Hoobastank.** (capo IX—but if I were you I would just play it open and sing along—it will sound great). We're going to call this a One-Six-Four-Five. Don't worry about why, yet—the numbers refer to some simple music theory that we'll cover in a later class. Right now, just concentrate on leaving those pivot fingers down.

One-Six-Four-Five

① ② ③ ④ etc.

|: G | Em | C | D7 :|

THE C MAJOR CHORD
Once you've got the C down, you're well on your way to playing with comfort and confidence.

Play the exact same progression only with two chords per measure (two beats per chord) and you'll be strumming **The Marcels'** version of **"Blue Moon"** (open), **"Stay Just A Little Bit Longer" by Jackson Browne** (open), **"Crazy" by Aerosmith** (capo II), and **"Complicated" by Avril Lavigne** (capo X but just play it open).

One-Six-Four-Five Split Measures

① ② ③ ④

|: G Em | C D7 :|

Here's a common variant of the G-Em-C-D7 progression heard in songs like **"Every Breath You Take"** by the **Police** (capo I) and **Ben E. King's** timeless **"Stand By Me."** (capo II and covered by **John Lennon** and **Seal** among others.) Notice you're playing the C and D7 for one measure each, but every other chord for two measures consecutively.

THE D SEVENTH CHORD
Use the first finger on the second string at the first fret to pivot between D7 and its good friend, C.

One-Six-Four-Five Stretched

① ② ③ ④ etc.

|: G | G | Em | Em |

| C | D7 | G | G :|

Play the same progression only beginning with C to get a pattern heard in **Coldplay's "Viva la Vida"** (capo I), **Joe Satriani's "If I Could Fly"** (capo V) or part of the chorus to **Van Morrison's "Brown Eyed Girl"** (open).

Four-Five-One-Six

① ② ③ ④ etc.

|: C | D7 | G | Em :|

Now play your favorite G-Em-C-D7 song—or just write your own! Remember, you only need a capo if you are playing along with the actual song recording. You can always sing and play any song on your own without a capo.

CLASS ____ PRACTICE CHART: ______________________________

Your teacher will assign you something great to fill in on this page! (If you're studying this book on your own, then use this page as a worksheet to figure out and write down an entire song you'd like to practice, or just write your own if you prefer.)

RHYTHM: | 1 + 2 + 3 + 4 + |

PRACTICE TAB, LICK or RIFF

T
A
B

New York City Guitar School
is HERE.

1 After 20 years in New York City, I am still impressed by all the tall buildings. NYC Guitar School's 11th floor balcony is a convenient perch for admiring them. We're located in the Recording and Rehearsal Arts Building on West 30th street, along with about 30 other music-related businesses.

2 NYC Guitar School teacher Tom demonstrates that the proper technique for holding a guitar includes an expression of enjoyment.

3 If you visit New York City Guitar School get ready to be smiled at. Jen (center) runs the school. She has a degree in Geology, which means she is well versed in all forms of rock. If you call up the school, you'll probably be warmly greeted by Genifer (left). This picture must have been taken on a Tuesday, because that is the day that Austin (right) takes a recovery from his eight hours of daily guitar playing and teaching to answer phones.

4 Here are a couple brand new Guitar for Absolute Beginner students. It looks like Matt W. is showing Richard and Laura how to play an A7 chord. Good luck, new students! (Matt just opened up Boston School of Guitar. If you're in Boston, check it out!)

5 Are these students so excited because they are about to take their guitar lesson? Or are they simply exhilarated to have survived our notoriously decrepit elevator? (Repairs are almost complete, so you may not get to experience the thrill that Tom, Dave, and Mika are feeling in this picture.)

CLASS

4

The Secret to Playing Great Rhythm Guitar PLUS the Small Barre— Gateway to Future Guitar Greatness

~ by Dan Emery of NYC Guitar School ©2009 ~

Lock your hand with the beat;
how to count eighth notes and more licks.

YOU ARE SMOKING: That's right, you're a smoking ball of guitar fire! You can play D, G, A7, Em, C and D7. Here's a picture of thousands bowing before you!

Now, let's learn a new rhythm! Right now, you're good at quarter-note strums. They're called that because there are four of them in the typical measure, just like there are four quarters in the typical dollar. And you're good, I hope, at tapping your foot once per beat and strumming down with your hand just as your foot taps down. You are, right?

We can represent this rhythm that you already know like this:

Down	Down	Down	Down
①	②	③	④

Or instead of using the word "down," we could use the official guitarist symbol for down, which is "⊓" = down strum.

So we could rewrite that rhythm like this:

⊓	⊓	⊓	⊓
①	②	③	④

Now, I have a crazy question for you. If you strum down, and then you strum down again, what direction is your hand going **between** those down strums?

If you said "up," then give yourself 25 gold stars, because you are right. What goes all the way down must come up before it can go down again. We guitarists identify the moment when your hand is coming up as being "off the beat." So **on the beat** you strum down, and **off the beat** you lift your hand up to get ready to strum again. There are four beats, so there are four off-beats. This makes a total of eight, so you could describe what we will learn in this lesson as **eighth-note strumming.** Since this involves swinging your hand up and down, we could also call this strum the **swing strum** or **alternate strumming.**

To get the idea of this, let's first **count aloud** as you tap your foot. On the beat, as you tap down, say "one" or whatever the number is. Off the beat, when you lift your foot, say "and," which will be written as "+." Really try to **feel** the beat, as you tap your foot. **Feel** the heaviness of the beat. Do this for several measures in a row, until you're comfortable and confident counting aloud with your foot tap.

You say:	"one"	"and"	"two"	"and"	"three"	"and"	"four"	"and"
The count is:	①	⊕	②	⊕	③	⊕	④	⊕
With your foot:	tap	lift	tap	lift	tap	lift	tap	lift

Now it is time for actual eighth-note strums! Grab your guitar and make a chord—a G chord, let's say. Count aloud and tap your foot. Each time you say a number, strum **down**: That's the downbeat. Each time you say "and," strum **up**, it's the upbeat. Above each count I've written the official guitar symbols for down (⊓) and up (V).

⊓ V ⊓ V ⊓ V ⊓ V
① ⊕ ② ⊕ ③ ⊕ ④ ⊕
| **G** |

Don't worry about the exact number of strings you hit with your up strum. You don't need to hit all the strings—just make sure you catch a few. Keep a nice, loose feeling in your arm and hand as you strum. Most importantly, feel the beat. Strum **down, on** the beat, and strum **up, off** the beat.

Play through the measure of eighth notes a few times, until you feel confident and comfortable. This technique is also called alternate strumming because you **alternate between** down and up strums.

Now try the D chord.

⊓ V ⊓ V ⊓ V ⊓ V
① ⊕ ② ⊕ ③ ⊕ ④ ⊕
| **D** |

This one is a little trickier because it's only 4 strings. But persevere: If Keith Richards learned to do it, so can you!

Understanding ON and OFF the beat is very important. For the rest of your guitar career, you'll be playing extremely complicated alternating strum patterns based on this fundamental precept:

The secret to playing great rhythm guitar is to move your hand with the beat.

Usually this means: ON the beat, strum DOWN and OFF the beat, strum UP.

Changing in Rhythm

Now we're going to play this rhythm as we change chords—from an Em to a G, let's say. We'll discuss this further. But first, give it a try. Count yourself in, tap your foot, and play:

⊓ V ⊓ V ⊓ V ⊓ V ⊓ V ⊓ V ⊓ V ⊓ V
① ⊕ ② ⊕ ③ ⊕ ④ ⊕ ① ⊕ ② ⊕ ③ ⊕ ④ ⊕
|: **Em** | **G** :|

At first, you probably won't be able to make your chord change exactly between the very last up strum of the G and the very first down strum of the Em.

Good guitar players begin moving to the next chord DURING the "and of four," so that they can cleanly finger the new chord on the next "one." That's taking care of JOB ONE, the most important part of guitar playing—which is playing the chord right on the beat. KEEP YOUR STRUM HAND MOVING no matter what, down on the downbeat and up on the offbeat. Then you change chords AS you strum.

Let's try that change again. I've put three asterisks below the "and of four" to remind you to begin changing chords there.

⊓ V ⊓ V ⊓ V ⊓ V ⊓ V ⊓ V ⊓ V ⊓ V
① ⊕ ② ⊕ ③ ⊕ ④ ⊕ ① ⊕ ② ⊕ ③ ⊕ ④ ⊕
|: **Em** *** | **G** *** :|

Got that? An excellent way to master this rhythm will be to pick a pair of chords and strum your way back and forth between them, before jumping into a song. Here are some nice pairs:

G-Em Em-C C-D7 D7-G D-G D-A7 G-A7

The Small Barre, Gateway to Future Greatness

Let's look ahead in your career as a guitar player. Here you are, learning lots of great chords and great songs, becoming comfortable with your "axe," and playing up a storm. But speaking of storms, there is a one lurking out there in the future. It is called the "barre chord," or more often it is called "the @*#^! barre chord!" It is the technique which separates the guitar players from the guitar weenies. Many times in my career as a guitar teacher I have picked up the ringing telephone only to hear a sobbing voice on the other line. With effort I'll be able to make out the words "finger," "pain" and "help, please, help" and I know that yet again someone is calling for assistance with barre chords.

Q: *Dan, what is a barre chord?*
A: A barre chord is a chord in which one finger, usually the first, holds down more than one string at the same time—sometimes even four or five!

I have good news for you–that crying, sobbing, disheartened guitar player pleading for barre chord help will not be you! Why not? Because my fellow teachers at the New York City Guitar School and I have discovered that by teaching the "small barre" well ahead of the "big barre" we can ensure that students smoothly and comfortably play barre chords like the complete and natural guitar demigods they are. So even though you won't learn the actual barre chord for some time, maybe even a few months, let's lay the foundation right now.

Let's examine the small barre more closely by trying one out. The small barre requires you to hold down two strings, the first and the second, with your first finger. Take your guitar in hand and place your first finger down flat on the first two strings at the first fret, as close to the fret as possible. Here is a helpful picture:

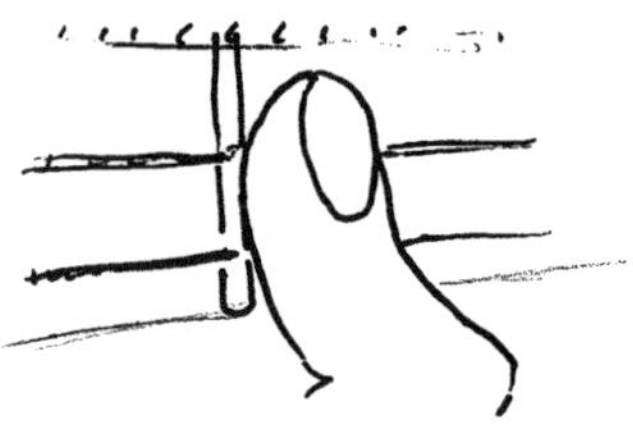

Note that the first finger is locked out at the first joint. Note also that the knuckles of the fretting hand are forward. Try the small barre a few times, and strum each of the strings to make sure that you are holding them down cleanly. Be patient—this usually takes a little practice! The muscle for this technique comes from the palm and the thicker part of your finger, with a little help from your thumb. By the way, I know that one of the fundamental great habits of playing guitar is to use your fingertips but a barre is a different technique. Use the padded part of the end of your first finger, nice and flat.

The best way to practice the small barre is to use it to play famous licks. The small barre appears in countless songs, differing only in the fret where it is played and the rhythm. In fact, a significant percentage of whatever hits happen to be on the radio at this very moment use this move. It is one of the fundamental techniques of a great lead guitar player.

Small Barre Lick # 1

This is a small-barre lick reminiscent of the first single-note guitar line heard in "Smells Like Teen Spirit" by Nirvana, and it's a fun way to practice your small barre. Several months from now you'll really need to use a barre for an advanced "big barre chord" and you'll be very happy that you practiced this. So put your first finger down flat on the first and second strings, nice and close to the fret, and try it out. Play down on the second string/first beat, and up on the first string/"and of one".

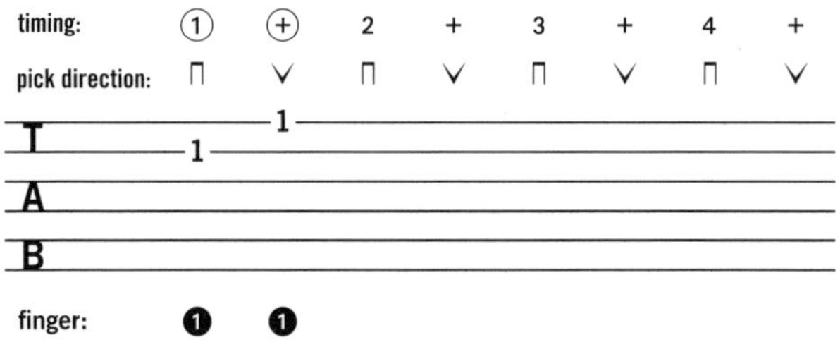

Small Barre Lick # 2

Try turning that guitar line into an exercise. On the first beat you'll pick down and then up on the second string. On the second beat you'll pick down and then up on the first string. And so on!

```
timing:          1   +   2   +   3   +   4   +
pick direction:  ⊓   V   ⊓   V   ⊓   V   ⊓   V
T  ----------------------1---1-----------1---1-
   ---------1---1-------------1---1------------
A  --------------------------------------------
   --------------------------------------------
B  --------------------------------------------
   --------------------------------------------
finger:          1   1   1   1   1   1   1   1
```

The Classic Sliding Small Barre

This lick has been used in a thousand songs and a half-million solos! I first learned it in "Johnny B. Goode" by Chuck Berry. It begins with a slide, which is indicated by the symbol /. In a slide, you place your finger at one fret and strum, and then you slide your finger to another fret as the first note is still ringing. In this case, begin with a small barre on the fourth fret. Then, as you pick the two strings, slide your small barre to the fifth fret, keeping pressure down on the strings. Then you'll strum the small barre at the fifth fret twice more.

We're going to play this lick with a rhythm called a **triplet**, because there are three notes packed into one beat. We'll need to count this a little differently than we've counted before. Now we'll say "**one**-trip-let-**two**-trip-let-**three**-trip-let-**four**-trip-let" to count a full measure. The entire lick is packed into the first beat.

```
timing:          1    trip  let   2  trip  let   3  trip  let   4  trip  let
pick direction:  ⊓ sl  ⊓     ⊓
T  ------4/5-5---5-----------------------------------------
   ------4/5-5---5-----------------------------------------
A  --------------------------------------------------------
   --------------------------------------------------------
B  --------------------------------------------------------
   --------------------------------------------------------
finger:          1 etc.
```

Licks are often like chords in that they are set moves that are combined by skilled guitarists in new and expressive ways. Just as many different artists use a G major chord in their songs, so do artists as divergent as ZZ Top, Nirvana, the White Stripes and Metallica all use the small barre in their songs.

THE SMALL BARRE
Note how flat the first finger is. This move is used constantly in lead guitar solos, plus it is the foundation for barre chords, which will come in very handy in your future guitar career.

One of the most common intro and solo moves in rock is to play the sliding small barre triplet, as above, then continuing to play the fifth-fret small barre over and over. You can hear this move in songs like "Revolution" by The Beatles and "Dust My Broom" by Elmore James. The slide only takes place on the first beat. On the beats two, three and four just play the small barre with triplet down strokes (two-trip-let, three-trip-let, four-trip-let). Try to smoothly repeat the entire measure four times in a row:

The Classic Sliding Small Barre #2

```
timing:          1    trip  let   2   trip  let   3   trip  let   4   trip  let
pick direction:  ⊓ sl  ⊓     ⊓     ⊓    ⊓     ⊓     ⊓    ⊓     ⊓     ⊓    ⊓     ⊓
T  ------5/6---6-----6-----6----6-----6-----6----6-----6-----6----6-----6---
   ------5/6---6-----6-----6----6-----6-----6----6-----6-----6----6-----6---
A  -------------------------------------------------------------------------
   -------------------------------------------------------------------------
B  -------------------------------------------------------------------------
   -------------------------------------------------------------------------
finger:          1 etc.
```

FUNDAMENTAL HABITS OF A GOOD GUITAR PLAYER

GOOD GUITARISTS KNOW THAT PLAYING IN RHYTHM IS MOST IMPORTANT!

The secret to playing great rhythm guitar is to move your hand with the beat. Usually this means: ON the beat, strum DOWN. OFF the beat, strum UP.

GOOD GUITARISTS ARE EFFICIENT. LEAVE FINGERS DOWN WHENEVER POSSIBLE —PIVOT, PIVOT, PIVOT!

USE YOUR FINGERTIP TO FRET NOTES, ALMOST BUT NOT QUITE ON THE FRET.

STRUM EFFICIENTLY, USING REST STROKES.

WHEN CHANGING CHORDS, MOVE THE MOST IMPORTANT FINGER FIRST.

ALWAYS PLAY THE OPTIMUM NUMBER OF STRINGS IN A CHORD.

PERCEIVE AND REMEMBER PATTERNS IN MUSIC!

Practice Suggestions for Class Four

- ✓ Warm up by playing your small barre licks. Then play your licks from Classes Two and Three.
- ✓ Play your Class Four song incessantly and smoothly and repeatedly. Sing along—download the mp3 or buy a CD if you aren't familiar with the words.
- ✓ Play all the way through your other songs.

My First Guitar

Many people learn to play guitar on a borrowed instrument. Jimi Hendrix did, and so did I. My first guitar actually belonged to the father of my best friend, Ted, back in the rural North Idaho country where I grew up.

It was perhaps inevitable that Ted and I would become best friends. We had a lot of important qualities in common, including:

1. We were the only two boys in our entire high school class who did not chew tobacco.
2. We were the only two boys in our entire high school class who took Physics.
3. Nobody else wanted to be seen with us.

Ted lived on a farm high above the Potlatch River canyon. His father, Robert, was a thick, strong and frugal farmer of wheat and lentils who rose early each morning for a focused 12 or 14 hours of work in the fields before returning to the house to relax before bedtime with some accounting or minor repair jobs. Ironically, he was allergic to wheat, and during the harvest season I mostly remember him as one big red inflammation. The dual intensity of his allergy and work ethic were matched by his shrewd love of bargains and his careful hoarding of any item that someday might prove useful under some scenario, no matter how unlikely.

(In the close environs of a New York City apartment, such an attitude could prove dangerous. For example, I recently read about a guy in the Bronx who saved everything until one of the narrow passageways through his apartment collapsed, trapping him. Luckily, after several days he was able to reach his phone and call for help. As an industrious farmer living on several hundred acres, Robert did not worry about being trapped by his stockpile of potentially useful items, although he did build several more barns in his spare time.)

Sometimes Robert's bargain hunting came in handy for me. For example, Ted, his brother Jed, my brother Luke and I all shared a love of Coca-Cola. One day, Robert took us all to the supermarket with a stack of coupons for cases of Coca-Cola for some unbelievably low price. He sent us in and out of the store with coupons and five-dollar bills until the car was completely full. When I said, "Uh, where are we going to sit on the way back?" he didn't even bother to answer. He gave each of us teenagers an extra case to carry on the five-mile walk back home. In an effort to lighten our load we drank as many cans as we could, but it made the trip much longer because soon we were forced to stop every 50 yards to relieve ourselves. Also, we had to tie the empty cans up in our shirts because we knew Robert would insist that they be returned for the nickel deposit.

Anyway, I digress, because this story is about my first guitar. The story actually begins a very long time ago, before I was born, when the young man who would become Ted's father saw an unbelievably good deal on a cheap acoustic guitar in a department store that was going out of business. He laid down his 12 dollars and took the guitar home to this conversation with his young wife, which I have made up on account of not being there:

Roz: "Now what did you go and buy that for, Bob? You're never going to use it!"
Robert: "This will come in handy one day. You'll see."

Then Robert carefully placed the guitar in the corner of one of his first barns, along with some other things which might very well come in handy one day, like a coffee can full of bent nails and the driver-side door from a 1934 International one-ton pickup truck.

Years passed. The sun rose and set. The earth turned from day into night. Each morning, Robert woke up and worked like a force of nature, farming, building and occasionally fathering sons, pausing only to stockpile useful items. Week by week such items were placed in the barn, layer upon layer, like sediments being deposited onto the bottom of a prehistoric sea.

Then, after a long time, I, Dan Emery, was born, mostly grew up, and became extremely interested in becoming a rock star. I had a great band name, which I will not reveal except under medieval torture. I also had a great band—Ted would be the singer, his brother Jed would be the drummer, my brother Luke would be the keyboard player, and I would be the guitar player. (A bass player was deemed unnecessary.) I even had my band's first write-up in the paper thanks to a gullible reporter on a tight deadline.

Clearly, the only thing standing between me and stardom was the fact that I lacked a guitar. Ted and Jed apparently mentioned this at home because one morning they told me that their father not only had a guitar, but he would lend it to me for as long as I wanted, as soon as he found it.

Two months later, I held my first guitar in my hands. The strings were brittle with age, the neck was bowed, and the first time I tried to tune it one of the tuners fell off, but I loved it. I practiced for two hours the first day, two hours the second day, and then I built up from there.

Each time I attempted to tune the guitar, I tightened the strings a little more and the neck of the guitar warped a little more under the tension, until the strings were almost impossible to push down against the frets. One day I heard a creaking sound from the corner of the room where the guitar was leaning. Right before my astonished eyes, the guitar convulsed like an tasered python, and then the neck snapped off with a dramatic crack and twang.

"Ted," I said, "the guitar broke."

"That's no problem," he replied. "We have a shop."

Ted and Jed had been fixing farm equipment since an early age and considered no repair job beyond them. They saw their mission as two-fold: first, to reattach the neck of the guitar to the body, and secondly to render it impervious to future breakage. They put metal plates on the neck and body, then connected them with a thick metal brace on each side of the neck with the same care and attention to durability they used when repairing plows. They even welded it to be sure nothing came loose. When I got the guitar back, there was so much steel plate on it that I had to squat to lift it. Also, it could never be tuned again. It was great, especially since I wanted to play heavy-metal guitar anyway.

In conclusion, I want to publicly thank Robert for giving me my first guitar, and to applaud his foresight in stockpiling it for my future use. If aliens invade, if a gigantic volcanic explosion plunges the world into three years of winter, if there is a major meteor impact, etc., etc., I will immediately depart New York City and head for the barns that contain the solution to any problem that may arise. I will leave you with another imagined conversation between Robert and Roz:

Robert: "I told you that guitar would come in handy one day."
Roz: "Oh, Bob—have another Coke."

CLASS FOUR SONGS

G-D-Em-C/Em-C-G-D Alt Strums   D-A7-G-A7 Alt Strums & Split Measures

You are building up some serious guitar-playing firepower, and you are now ready to learn one of the most mind-blowingly popular chord progressions of all time. Using this progression you can play hundreds or thousands of songs, including: **"Swing, Swing" by The All-American Rejects** (open), **"Don't Matter" by Akon** (capo II), **"Far Away" by Nickelback** (capo IV), **"My Name Is Jonas" by Weezer** (capo IV), **"Down, Down, Down" by Bruce Springsteen** (capo II) and many others. We'll see more of much more of this intensely powerful progression in future classes. In the meantime, pick your favorite G-D-Em-C song, adjust a capo as needed, and play along with the band.

Remember, keep your strum hand moving!

Mind Blowing Progression in G

⊓ ∨ ⊓ ∨ ⊓ ∨ ⊓ ∨
① + ② + ③ + ④ + etc.
|: G | D | Em | C :|

Songs will often be driven by the same chords played in the same order, but starting on a different chord in the progression. For example if we play the progression from the top of this page, but simply start on the E minor instead of the G, we'll be playing the underlying harmony for '90s rock anthems like practically all of **The Cranberries' "Zombie"** (open) and practically all of **The Smashing Pumpkins' "Disarm"** (open).

90s Rock Anthem

⊓ ∨ ⊓ ∨ ⊓ ∨ ⊓ ∨
① + ② + ③ + ④ + etc.
|: Em | C | G | D :|

In all the excitement of playing C chords, do you remember that A7 chord? I hope so, because here is a classic D-A7-G-A7 repeating pattern. Please note that the chords change every two beats—that means that for every chord, you'll get a down-up-down-up.

KEEP YOUR HAND MOVING, even when you are changing chords. This pattern can be discerned in songs like **"First Cut" by Cat Stevens** (covered famously by Sheryl Crow, open), the verse to **"All Star" by Smash Mouth** (capo IV) and most of **"Small Town" by John Cougar** (capo IX) and **"Love Stinks" by the J. Geils Band** (capo X). Depending on the song you might need to vary your strum. As always, get the song, LISTEN, and try to play along. I recommend trying the **Sheryl Crow** version of **"First Cut"** to begin with. If you don't have the song, buy it, listen carefully and then try playing along. Here's a practice progression entitled "You Are A First Cut All-Star".

You Are A First Cut All-Star

⊓ ∨ ⊓ ∨ ⊓ ∨ ⊓ ∨
① + ② + ③ + ④ + etc.
|: D A7 | G A7 :|

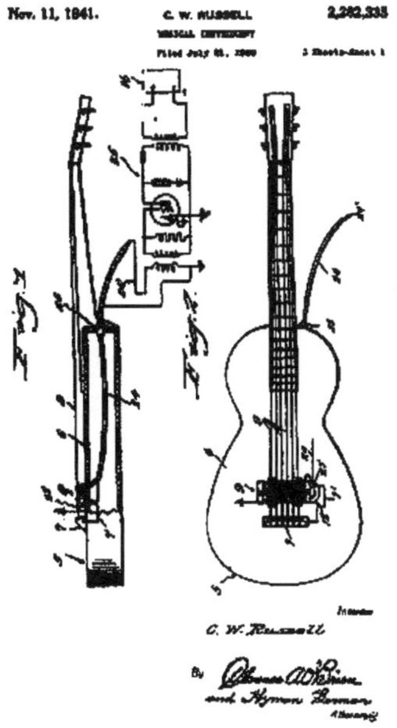

CLASS ____ PRACTICE CHART: ______________________________

Your teacher will assign you something great to fill in on this page! (If you're studying this book on your own, then use this page as a worksheet to figure out and write down an entire song you'd like to practice, or just write your own if you prefer.)

RHYTHM: | 1 + 2 + 3 + 4 + |

PRACTICE TAB, LICK or RIFF

T
A
B

CLASS

5

The Gentle Art of Riffing PLUS A minor (The Saddest Chord)

~ by Dan Emery of NYC Guitar School ©2009 ~

{ *How to count and play riffs; planting fingers to change between G, C and D; A minor.* }

Master the Gentle Art of Riffing through Basic Counting

Black Sabbath! AC/DC! Metallica! Joan Jett! Besides a propensity for wearing black, these artists and many others share a tendency to not strum in a folksy manner. Instead, they "riff" on chords. A riff is a set of chords or notes played in a short and memorable pattern. Think of the introductions to "Smoke on the Water" by Deep Purple or the main guitar part to "Smells Like Teen Spirit" by Nirvana.

There is no better first-chord riff than the one used as the backbone for more songs than probably any other riff in existence. I am going to call it the "Wild Thing" riff, even though the exact same riff can be used to play "Walking on Sunshine" by Katrina and the Waves, the chorus to "All Star" by Smash Mouth and hundreds or even thousands of other songs. We're going to learn this riff in the key of G, using open chords. (A "key" is a way in which skilled guitarists perceive order in music—you'll learn about keys in just a few lessons!)

First let's learn the G chord part. Count yourself in using eighth notes ("one and two and, etc.") and then boldly strum the G chord on "one" and "two". Remember that "⊓" means "strum down."

```
⊓     ⊓
①  +  ②  +  3  +  4  +     1  +  2  +  3  +  4  +
|:G   G                |                        :|
```

Now let's turn this into almost a riff. We're going to do something we've never done before: We're going to play a down strum OFF the beat on the "AND."

So now, very slowly, count and play the full first measure until you can do so in a reasonably confident manner four times through. Try to lead with your third finger when changing to the C chord.

```
⊓     ⊓           ⊓  ⊓
①  +  ②  +  3  ⊕  ④  +     1  +  2  +  3  +  4  +
|:G   G        C  C    |                        :|
```

Next, learn the second measure of the riff. You'll strum with the exact same timing, only now going from D to C. Again, do this until you can play in a reasonably confident manner four times in a row. Try to lead with your third finger when changing to the C chord.

```
                           ⊓     ⊓           ⊓  ⊓
1  +  2  +  3  +  4  +     ①  +  ②  +  3  ⊕  ④  +
|:                     |   D     D        C  C  :|
```

...at in both measures, the C chord is ...PATED. In other words, instead of changing ... playing ON the third beat, we play it OFF the third beat, or on the "and of three." This syncopation is the key to making "Wild Thing" and the various other songs built on this riff sound like they should.

Now, here comes the entire riff. Count and play slowly until you get the hang of this riff. Good finger plants will be extremely helpful when making these fast, syncopated changes. When changing to G plant the second finger. When changing to C plant the third finger. When changing to D, plant the first finger.

THE WILD RIFF!

⊓ ⊓ ⊓ ⊓ ⊓ ⊓ ⊓ ⊓

(1) + (2) + 3 (+) (4) + (1) + (2) + 3 (+) (4) +

‖: G G C C | D D C C :‖

Now, Learn this Chord to Make Your Listeners Weep with Raw, Ragged Emotion!

It is time for another emotional, poignant minor chord, the very famous A-minor chord. In the movie "Spinal Tap," a Nigel Tufnel proclaims that D minor is, in fact, the saddest chord. But many take issue with this analysis, considering A minor to be even sadder. Below is a diagram of the A-minor chord, often written as "Am".

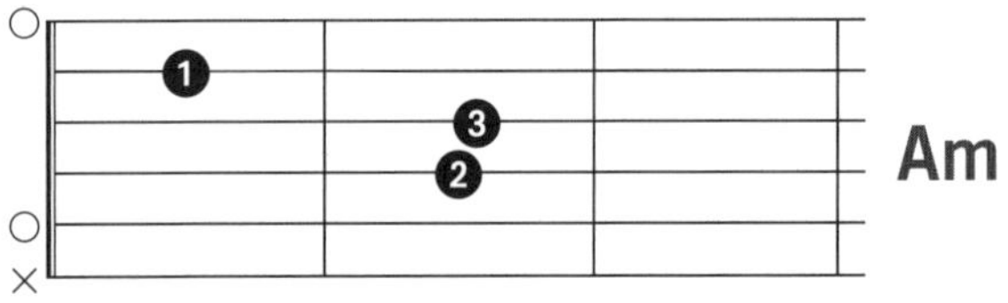

I've heard people say that we think of major chords as "happy" and minor chords as "sad" simply through association—if you see enough movies of weeping people with a minor chord playing in the background, after a while a minor chord makes you want to cry, goes this argument. I think this is untrue—somehow the mathematics of the vibrations involved in a minor chord just resonate in a particular way with humans. For example, I was listening to some classical music in a minor key with my 2-year-old son, and he said, "Dada, the violins are lonely." He knew, without being told.

The A-minor chord is often used with the C-major chord. What an easy change! You only have to move your third finger, and you strum five strings on each of the chords. Practice this change until you are reasonably comfortable and confident.

⊓ ⊓ ⊓ ⊓ ⊓ ⊓ ⊓ ⊓

(1) + (2) + (3) + (4) + (1) + (2) + (3) + (4) +

‖: C | Am :‖

Your plant finger on the A minor is the second finger. In other words, when fingering this chord, begin with the second finger before adding the other two. Try changing between Am and G (six strings and also a second-finger plant) and then between Am and D (four strings and a first-finger plant) to get more comfortable with A minor.

⊓ ⊓ ⊓ ⊓ ⊓ ⊓ ⊓ ⊓
① + ② + ③ + ④ + ① + ② + ③ + ④ +
|: **G** | **A**m :|

⊓ ⊓ ⊓ ⊓ ⊓ ⊓ ⊓ ⊓
① + ② + ③ + ④ + ① + ② + ③ + ④ +
|: **D** | **A**m :|

A Minor Catastrophe

Speaking of A minor, I once taught one of the worst guitar lessons in my life with an A-minor-laden song, "Knockin' on Heaven's Door." Back before New York City Guitar School existed, I used to hold open "anti-procrastination" sessions in my apartment in Williamsburg, Brooklyn. I'd invite my illustrator/writer/thesis-writing/etc. friends over to drink coffee and work on whatever we'd been putting off. If I had a guitar lesson I'd go into the other room to teach my student.

Nigel Tufnel Proclaims that D Minor is, in Fact, the Saddest Chord. But Many Take Issue with this Analysis, Considering A Minor to be Even Sadder.

One day my friend Alia came over. Alia's cool—she hammers nails into her nose, eats glass, and lies on beds of nails. as "Vulvina, Queen of Nails." But on this day she was just Alia, professional illustrator and badly in need of some concentrated drawing to meet an impending deadline. In she came, and she said, "Dan, how is it going?"

"Well," I said, "it's going great except that there's this song that's driving me nuts. It's 'Knockin' on Heaven's Door,' and I keep teaching it to people because it's the best song for learning A minor. But lately, every time I'm playing the song, I feel like darkness is closing in around me, and I feel like I've done nothing for my entire life except sing and play 'Knockin' on Heaven's Door,' and I think 'Is this it? Is this my life? Will this always be my life?' I've got to stop teaching that song, because if I do it one more time I'm going to jump out the window!"

Just then the doorbell rang. Alia retreated to the other room and began drawing furiously, and I went to the door. "Hi Lisa," I said, and in came Lisa, a gifted Broadway dancer and a brand-new-guitarist. We settled down with our guitars and she said "I'm so excited to learn 'Knockin' on Heaven's Door' today."

There was a single, loud and suddenly suppressed snort of laughter from the other room, and I began to laugh uncontrollably. In fact, I couldn't stand up!

"What's so funny?" Lisa asked. "Oh, nothing," I said, and we went on with the lesson, except that approximately each verse I'd start laughing again. Poor Lisa! Honesty is always the best policy, and I should have told her the full story; in retrospect she must have thought I was laughing at her, or perhaps that I was under the influence of some laugh-inducing substance! She never came back, even though she showed great promise as a guitarist. I remember that lesson with great shame as a teacher. On the other hand, ever since then I've loved to teach "Knockin' on Heaven's Door"!

The first time I heard "Knockin' on Heaven's Door," it was by Guns n' Roses. I liked it! A few months later I heard a very different version by Eric Clapton. I said, "Wow! Guns n' Roses are bigger than I thought—I can't believe that Eric Clapton covered one of their songs!" When I tried to impress an attractive girl with this piece of information, she informed me of what you already know: Bob Dylan wrote the song. Years later Avril Lavigne released her own version, and across America right now there are millions of people who think she wrote it! Sometimes I'll give a class a choice between learning an unnamed song by Clapton, Guns n' Roses, or Avril Lavigne. We'll discuss the pros and cons, and hopefully the discussion will become spirited. Then we take a vote, after which I reveal that we'll be learning a song made famous by all three artists.

Let's Review Some of the Fundamental Principles of Guitar Playing.

You are doing quite well in your musical endeavor. You've learned to play chords and songs, and you are building the habits of a skilled guitar player. Most importantly, you recognize **that there is only one way to learn to play guitar—and that is to practice!** The more faithfully you pick up your guitar to play, the greater will be your enjoyment and mastery. In fact, the practicing is itself a large part of the playing; the journey is the end.

When you form a chord with your fretting hand, you habitually **use your fingertips,** and you **finger close to the frets.** This allows you to expend the least amount of energy with the maximum results when fingering chords. Speaking of fretting-hand efficiency, you **leave fingers down when possible** while changing chords—this is called pivoting. Also, you **put the most important finger down first**—we call this finger the plant finger. With your strumming hand, you **consistently play the optimum number of strings;** your hand plays from the root note of any given chord.

You know that **music is made up of patterns.** You look for these patterns when you learn new songs, and doing so helps you to **learn songs by heart.**

Finally, you recognize that the key element of sounding great is to **play in rhythm.** Therefore, you tap your foot and you **lock your strumming hand in with the beat.** Furthermore, when changing chords you always **hit the new chord right on the beat.**

Practice Suggestions for Class Five

✓ **Begin by playing the Wild Riff. Play the Wild Riff early, often and over and over—it is laying the groundwork for next week's lesson. PLAY LOTS OF WILD RIFF!**

✓ **Play entire songs all the way through. Play Knocking, You Are A First Cut All-Star, and any other songs you have learned. Try singing!**

✓ **Finish by playing all your licks.**

TRY TO PRACTICE AT LEAST THREE TIMES THIS WEEK!

CLASS FIVE SONGS

G-C-D-C The Wild Riff G-D-Am-C Alt Strums

If you want to write a hit rock song that makes people dance, I suggest you try working The Wild Riff into it. Very similar riffs drive songs such as **"Walking on Sunshine" by Katrina and The Waves** (capo III), the chorus to **"All Star" by Smash Mouth** (very inconvenient with a capo, but very convenient in the future when you know barre chords!), **"Get Off My Cloud" by The Rolling Stones** (ditto), **"Hang on Sloopy" by The McCoys** (no capo needed!), **"Wild Thing" by The Troggs** (capo II), and others.

The WILD Riff

```
⊓       ⊓           ⊓   ⊓       ⊓       ⊓           ⊓   ⊓
①   +   ②   +   3   ⊕   ④   +   ①   +   ②   +   3   ⊕   ④   +
|:G     G           C   C     | D       D           C   C      :|
```

The following killer chord progression can be used to play **"What You Meant" by Franz Ferdinand** (open), **"Roses From My Friends" by Ben Harper** (open), and most notably for guitar players, **"Knockin' on Heaven's Door" by Bob Dylan** (open, covered famously by **Eric Clapton, Avril Lavigne,** and of course **Guns N' Roses**). Try playing with alternate strums.

Proto-Knocking

```
⊓ V ⊓ V ⊓ V ⊓ V
① ⊕ ② ⊕ ③ ⊕ ④ ⊕ etc.
|:G        |D        |Am        |Am        :|
```

Of course, the C-major chord is THE key chord of beginning guitar. By adding a C to the end of the G-D-Am progression, we get the essential harmony behind **"Closing Time" by Semisonic** (open), **"Hot N Cold" by Katy Perry** (open), and much of **"These Girls" by Ryan Adams** (capo III) and **"'J' For Jules" by 'Til Tuesday** (capo III). Oh, and just play the same repeating four chords only starting on the Am to get **"Who Will Save Your Soul" by Jewel** (open). Remember to leave your first and second finger down when changing from Am to C—just reach out with your third finger!

THE A MINOR CHORD
Learn the A minor to make your listeners weep with raw, jagged emotion.

G to D to A Minor to C Time

```
⊓ V ⊓ V ⊓ V ⊓ V
① ⊕ ② ⊕ ③ ⊕ ④ ⊕ etc.
|:G          D         | Am          C          :|
```

Here's a practice progression including changes from D to A minor and also D to C, which I'm calling "Knocking" in honor of **"Knockin' On Heaven's Door."** As always, get a copy of whichever song you want to learn to play, listen to it carefully, and then try to play along with it. If you need help, ask a friend or classmate, or get the sheet music.

Knocking

```
⊓ V ⊓ V ⊓ V ⊓ V
① ⊕ ② ⊕ ③ ⊕ ④ ⊕ etc.
|:G         |D         |Am         |Am         |
| G         |D         |C          |C          :|
```

CLASS ____ PRACTICE CHART: ________________________________

Your teacher will assign you something great to fill in on this page! (If you're studying this book on your own, then use this page as a worksheet to figure out and write down an entire song you'd like to practice, or just write your own if you prefer.)

RHYTHM: | 1 + 2 + 3 + 4 + |

PRACTICE TAB, LICK or RIFF

T
A
B

CLASS

6

Rhythm 101: Learn This and Understand How Strums Work

~ by Dan Emery of NYC Guitar School ©2009 ~

{ *The powerful "basic strum" pattern* }

HAVE YOU EVER PLAYED air guitar? Have you played **blazing air lead guitar,** your fingers undulating like over-caffeinated garter snakes? You weren't sitting down, and you were having a good time, right?

Despite my years of intensive study of the actual guitar and hundreds of hours spent on stage playing actual guitar songs in front of actual people, I must admit that my greatest exploits came with my trusty air guitar in hand. Why, I can't even count the times that I casually tossed off a Chuck Berry solo note for note on my air Telecaster, often while simultaneously eating deep-fried potato products.

I achieved my greatest air-guitar triumphs as a "student" at the University of Idaho. I lived there for several years in a dormitory called Upham Hall, which featured a large communal shower room with six high-powered nozzles. Early in the morning, this room was occupied by a rotating cast of surly, hung-over young men. I, however, was not one of those worthy class-bound students, because staying up all night playing guitar and juggling made me too sleepy to get up before noon.

The Secret to Playing Great Rhythm Guitar is to Move Your Hand with the Beat.

Usually this means:
ON the beat, strum DOWN.
OFF the beat, strum UP.

Anyway, at two or three in my typical afternoon, I woke up and experienced a momentary pang of regret at having missed lunch. I generally decided to make the best of it. "I'll work on my air-guitar skills," I said to myself, heading off to the giant shower room.

Alone, I turned on all six showers full throttle and as hot as possible. The roar of the water cascading and echoing against the tiles sounded a lot like the open throated cries of forty thousand people screaming "EM-ER-Y, EM-ER-Y!" The rising steam quickly cut vision to just a few inches, much like six powerful fog machines. The large tiled floor provided me ample room to leap, slide and duck-walk, and the scarring jets of hot water aided me in concentrating fully on creating the ultimate air concert for my fans. Best of all, thanks to the University of Idaho's "physical plant" (whatever that is) the hot water never ran out. Sometimes it would be five or six in the afternoon by the time I staggered out into the hallway, pink and wrinkled and barely in time to get ready for juggling club.

Yes, those were good times, and I'm sure you can relate. But my point is, if you want to play guitar like a superstar, then you'd better work on your air-guitar skills!

Do you remember the secret to playing great rhythm guitar? It's locking your hand in with the beat.

For example, if you were to play a G chord with the alternate strums, on every beat you would strum down, and off every beat (on the "and") you would strum up. Try it:

⊓ V ⊓ V ⊓ V ⊓ V
① ⊕ ② ⊕ ③ ⊕ ④ ⊕
𝄆 G 𝄇

Wouldn't it feel great to strum complicated, tricky strum patterns which mixed down and up strums? You CAN strum those strums—but first you have to learn to lock your hand in with the beat so completely that it keeps moving exactly in rhythm regardless of the strum pattern that you are playing. In other words, you must learn to properly **air strum!**

Proper Air Strums

To properly air strum, move your hand up and down, down on the beat and up off the beat—without making a sound. Your hand will keep moving even if you are not actually hitting the strings of the guitar. This is vitally important! Make a G chord, count aloud and move your hand with the beat, but don't actually hit the strings of the guitar. To show this, I've written a measure complete with count and the strum direction. Move your hand with the beat:

⊓ V ⊓ V ⊓ V ⊓ V
1 + 2 + 3 + 4 +

Now let's practice articulating a strum here or there. Count aloud, move your hand with the beat, but only strum the indicated beat. It is important to place your air strums exactly in rhythm. Your hand will move DOWN on every beat and UP on every "and" and it will actually strum the strings only on "two."

⊓ V ⊓ V ⊓ V ⊓ V
1 + ② + 3 + 4 +
𝄆 G 𝄇

Now try a solitary off-beat, in this case the "and of two", which will be played with an up strum.

⊓ V ⊓ V ⊓ V ⊓ V
1 + 2 ⊕ 3 + 4 +
𝄆 G 𝄇

Play through this next measure several times. It's tricky! Keep your hand moving with the beat, and strum the indicated beats and off-beats. You know, if you were watching from a distance, each of these exercises would look exactly the same—the hand would just be moving steadily with the beat.

⊓ V ⊓ V ⊓ V ⊓ V
① + 2 ⊕ 3 ⊕ 4 +
𝄆 G 𝄇

The Basic Strum

Now you'll apply your new knowledge to an actual strum. I call it the basic strum, because it basically sounds great on just about any song. Keep your hand moving, including on the "and of one" and the "and of three" when you aren't actually strumming. Please try to make these air strums exactly with the count. You never need to speed your hand or slow your hand—everything will be where it is needed when it is needed. I've written in the pick direction only when you actually strum, because I know that you will remember to lift your hand up on the +'s.

⊓ ⊓ V ⊓ ⊓ V
① + ② ⊕ ③ + ④ ⊕
𝄆 **G** 𝄇

Some people call it the "Down, Down-Up, Down, Down-Up" strum, because that is how you do it. Others call it "The Country Strum" because it is used in so many country and folk songs. Play it until you begin to feel comfortable with it, then try changing chords as you strum.

Changing in Rhythm

Smoking! Okay, now we're going to play this rhythm as we change chords—from an Em to a G, so that we have that nice first-finger pivot to help us out. Count yourself in, tap your foot, and play:

⊓ ⊓ V ⊓ ⊓ V ⊓ ⊓ V ⊓ ⊓ V
① + ② ⊕ ③ + ④ ⊕ ① + ② ⊕ ③ + ④ ⊕
𝄆 **Em** | **G** 𝄇

After you've done that a few times in a row, try the basic strum with a plant change, D to G. Here I've written the rhythm out without the pick direction, because I know that on the beat your hand moves down, and off the beat your hand moves up! Play this change through until it feels moderately comfortable.

① + ② ⊕ ③ + ④ ⊕ ① + ② ⊕ ③ + ④ ⊕
𝄆 **D** | **G** 𝄇

Often beginning guitarists will say, "Hey, if I'm right-handed, why am I using my left hand for these tricky chords? Shouldn't I be using my very coordinated right hand for that?"

Left-handers will ask the same question except reversed.

Now you know the answer—the fretting hand merely SETS UP the music—it is the strumming hand that EXPRESSES the music! Therefore your dominant hand is the one that strums.

GOOD GUITARISTS KNOW THAT RHYTHM IS MOST IMPORTANT!

The secret to playing great rhythm guitar is to move your hand with the beat

WHETHER YOU'RE ACTUALLY STRUMMING OR NOT!

Usually this means: ON the beat, strum or (air strum) DOWN.

OFF the beat, strum or (air strum) UP.

FUNDAMENTAL HABITS OF A GOOD GUITAR PLAYER

GOOD GUITARISTS KNOW THAT PLAYING IN RHYTHM IS MOST IMPORTANT!

The secret to playing great rhythm guitar is to move your hand with the beat. Usually this means: ON the beat, strum DOWN. OFF the beat, strum UP.

GOOD GUITARISTS ARE EFFICIENT. LEAVE FINGERS DOWN WHENEVER POSSIBLE —PIVOT, PIVOT, PIVOT!

USE YOUR FINGERTIP TO FRET NOTES, ALMOST BUT NOT QUITE ON THE FRET.

STRUM EFFICIENTLY, USING REST STROKES.

WHEN CHANGING CHORDS, MOVE THE MOST IMPORTANT FINGER FIRST.

ALWAYS PLAY THE OPTIMUM NUMBER OF STRINGS IN A CHORD.

PERCEIVE AND REMEMBER PATTERNS IN MUSIC!

Practice Suggestions for Class Six

First and Third Practice Sessions:

✓ Warm up by playing the Wild Riff incessantly to get used to the G to C change.

✓ Then play your Class Four song incessantly to get used to changing chords as you continue strumming. Sing along!

✓ Review the basic strum, then play your Class Six song.

✓ Finish with concentrated Wild Riff practice.

Second Practice Session:

✓ Warm up by strumming through your Class Three and Class Five songs.

✓ Practice your Cool Licks.

✓ Review the basic strum, then play your Class Three and Class Five songs again, only this time using the basic strum.

✓ Play your Class Six song.

✓ Finish with concentrated Small Barre practice.

CLASS SIX SONGS
The Basic Strum

HERE'S A GREAT WARM-UP FOR YOU! Download **"Bells Ring" by Mazzy Star** and try to figure out how to play along with it using the basic strum and G and C. It is nice and mellow, and is great for practicing your G-to-C change with open chords. If that's too mellow for you, try something like **"Boss D.J." by Sublime** (open), or **"Wheat Kings" by The Tragically Hip** (also open). Or how about **"Every Morning" by Sugar Ray?** (You might have to put your capo on the first fret for that last one.)

Once you are feeling confident with your G to C change, go on to the basic strum with more chords. I first learned the next eight bars played with the basic strum in the context of **"Blowin' In The Wind" by Bob Dylan** (capo VII). Later I learned that the same harmony underlies **John Denver's "Leaving on a Jet Plane"** (open, and covered by **Peter, Paul and Mary** among others). This sequence will get you started on your way to basic-strum greatness. I'll call this exercise **"Leaves In The Wind"** in honor of the two aforementioned songs.

(By the way, if you want to play FAST, then get a copy of **"Tubthumping (I Get Knocked Down)" by Chumbawamba,** put your capo on the seventh fret, and try to adapt this progression for that song!)

The Most Basic G to C Song Ever

```
⊓       ⊓   V   ⊓       ⊓   V
①   +   ②   ⊕   ③   +   ④   ⊕   etc.
|: G                            | C                 :|
```

Leaves in the Wind

```
⊓     ⊓ V ⊓   ⊓ V
① + ② ⊕ ③ + ④ ⊕ etc.
|: G        | C        | G        | C        |
|  G        | C        | D        | D        |
|  G        | C        | G        | C        |
|  G        | C        | D        | D        :|
```

CLASS ____ PRACTICE CHART: ______________________________

Your teacher will assign you something great to fill in on this page! (If you're studying this book on your own, then use this page as a worksheet to figure out and write down an entire song you'd like to practice, or just write your own if you prefer.)

RHYTHM: | 1 + 2 + 3 + 4 + |

PRACTICE TAB, LICK or RIFF

T
A
B

String Theory
Events
method
Guitars
1

3

4

5

6

1 On the other hand, if you visit Brooklyn Guitar School, prepare to be greeted with ukuleles and juggling. This is Shane, who keeps a lot of things in the air while running the school!

2 Our bathroom is for both male guitar players and female guitar players.

3 Students waiting for their classes mix, mingle and make impromptu music in the school lounge. Meghan is standing with her guitar and Saurabh and Ellen are playing.

4 One of the doors in our lounge leads to Allan and Gotham Guitar Works. Here is Allan performing surgery on somebody's guitar.

5 The vast majority of NYC Guitar School students are adults, but we do have some younger players. Here Josh fingertaps the solo to "Beat It". Eliane, who runs our Teen Rock Guitar program, listens proundly. I'm proud, too—I taught Josh his very first lessons.

6 The students in this picture are actually taking a lead guitar class, not Absolute Beginners. I've included their picture for two reasons: first, they used to be beginners, so they are inspirational examples; second, their teacher, Suke, is one of the very first NYC Guitar School teachers. He's not in the picture, but you can see how pleased Gene, Matthew and Eric are. About half the faculty of our guitar school have taken lessons from Suke, includuing me.

CLASS

7

Learn the Best Strum and Always Sound Terrific

~ by Dan Emery of NYC Guitar School ©2009 ~

— SPECIAL CLASS TEN NOTE! —

Class Ten, which is your MASSIVE MOMENT OF GLORY, is coming up in just a few weeks. That's right—in Class Ten you will have the opportunity as a class to informally perform a song for an audience of several NYCGS staff and students as well as any friend or relative you wish to invite.

Q: *Who exactly is performing?*
A: Your entire class, including your teacher!

Q: *Should I feel nervous about this?*
A: Absolutely not. You'll have lots of company strumming, your audience will generally be fewer than five people, and they will be very friendly, too.

Q: *Why do we do this?*
A: At NYC Guitar School, we have found that students who play in front of others are massively more successful in playing guitar. Even just strumming a D chord in front of others forces you to achieve a higher level of mastery with the D chord and strumming. Playing in front of others is a breakthrough point as big as learning to change chords in rhythm!

Q: *Can I play a song by myself?*
A: Absolutely, if you would like to. Just let your teacher know!

Q: *How about with a friend or classmate?*
A: Absolutely!

Q: *Will I have to do this after every class I take here?*
A: Nope—just this course and a few electives which may be a year or two in your future.

Next Week You will Choose a Song to Play!

The basic strum sounds great and is used in many, many songs. But there is one strumming pattern which is used even more. In fact, this strum sounds so good that many people learn it and never bother to learn any other strum. At NYC Guitar School we call it "the best strum." Master the material in this lesson, and you'll have a strum that will make you sound like a pro on virtually every song for the rest of your life!

Let's review alternate strumming. First and most importantly, remember that:

The secret to playing great rhythm guitar is to move your hand with the beat.

Usually this means: ON the beat, strum DOWN. OFF the beat, strum UP.

Review air strums. Make a G chord, count aloud and move your hand with the beat, but don't actually hit the strings of the guitar. Move your hand with the beat!

⊓ V ⊓ V ⊓ V ⊓ V
1 + 2 + 3 + 4 +
| G |

Review articulating a strum here or there. Count aloud, move your hand with the beat, and strum the indicated beats for the next several exercises. Place your air strums exactly in rhythm. Your hand will move **down** on every beat and **up** on every "and" and will actually strum only on the circled beats. **Keep your hand moving even when you are not strumming!**

⊓ V ⊓
1 + (2) (+) 3 + (4) +
| G |

⊓ V
1 + (2) + 3 (+) 4 +
| G |

And here are several reviews of THE BASIC STRUM. I've included some redundant rhythm notation to subliminally prepare you for future musical exploits. Don't be alarmed!

(1) + (2) (+) (3) + (4) (+)
|: G :|

(1) + (2) (+) (3) + (4) (+) (1) + (2) (+) (3) + (4) (+)
|: Em | G :|

(1) + (2) (+) (3) + (4) (+) (1) + (2) (+) (3) + (4) (+)
|: D | G :|

The Best Strum

Begin building up to the full best-strum rhythm by air strumming your way into this bar. Repeat it a few times. **Keep your hand moving** on the 1 + 2 + 3. **Keep your hand moving with the beat whether or not you are actually strumming!**

V ⊓ V
1 + 2 + 3 (+) (4) (+)
| G |

Now leap into the best strum. Try it once through nice and slow. The key is: **move your hand down on the "three"** (even though you are not actually strumming!)

MOVE YOUR HANDS DOWN RIGHT HERE ON THE "THREE" SO THAT YOUR HAND WILL BE IN POSITION FOR THE UP STRUM.

⊓ ⊓ V ↓ V ⊓ V
(1) + (2) (+) 3 (+) (4) (+)
| G |

Then cycle through it. Some people call this the "Down, Down-Up, Up-Down-Up" strum, because that is how you do it. As long as your hand is moving with the beat, though, your hand will be moving in the right direction at the right time.

Play it until you begin to feel moderately comfortable before progressing to chord changes.

Best-Strumming with Chord Changes

Start with a pivot change—from an Em to a G. Tap your foot, count yourself in and play. You never need to speed your hand or slow your hand—everything will be where it is needed when it is needed. Remember to leave your first finger down on the fret while you change chords.

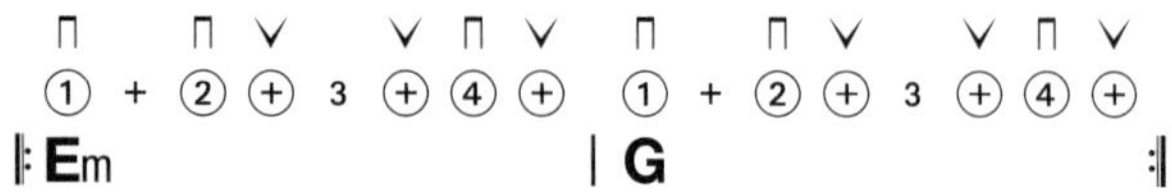

After you've done that a few times in a row, try the best strum with a plant change, G to C. Begin moving your fretting hand right after the "four" as you maintain your strum. It is the job of the chords to keep up with the strum because RHYTHM IS MOST IMPORTANT.

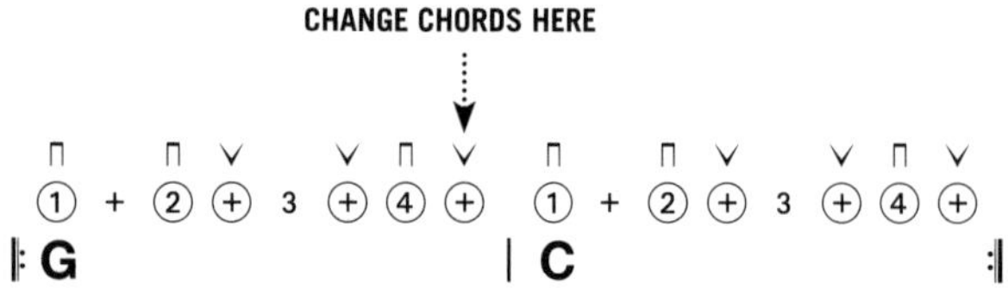

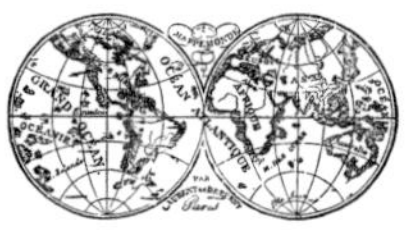

Sometimes it's Just Hard

Isn't it true that if you step back for a moment and take a clear-eyed look at where you are and where you've been, it is obvious that you have made massive progress in the art of guitar playing? Sometimes it is hard to maintain that perspective, though, when you're in the middle of trying to master yet another new and unusual guitar technique, rhythm or chord.

It's been about eight years since I put away my riding-in-a-van-hustling-guitar-slinging ways aside. Since then I have devoted myself to making learning guitar as absolutely accessible, achievable and easy for my students as possible. "It's easy to play guitar!" I shouted. "Anybody can learn to do it!" I strove to make every chord, every progression and every piece of theory as easy as possible.

But one day one of my teenage students came in and taught me a valuable lesson. He said, "Hey, Dan—I just realized something."

"What?" I asked.

"Sometimes guitar playing is just not easy" he explained. "Sometimes it's just hard, and you just have to keep working at it until you get it, and it takes a lot of time and effort."

I felt like I'd been hit by a thunderbolt. He was absolutely right. And in my effort to make guitar accessible to people, I'd actually been doing them a disservice by intimating that it was always easy to play guitar. No wonder my students sometimes got discouraged when it wasn't!

For example, for most beginning guitar players, the G to C change is a giant and inconvenient pain in the phalanges. Theoretically, it is easy to get comfortable with the change—after all, you simply need to practice the change somewhere between 1,000 and 2,000 times. But, practically, practicing changing from G to C between 1,000 and 2,000 times takes a lot of, uh, practice. And sometimes that's not easy!

The good news is that YOU CAN DO IT! And when you get tired, when your fingertips are sore, when you lose your focus, give yourself a pat on the back! In life and guitar playing alike, persevering may not always be easy—but you'll be glad when you can say "it was worth it!"

Practice Suggestions for Class Seven

This is an important week of practice! You are nearing the end of the course—this is a vital week for solidifying what you've learned so far, so that you can understand new concepts in the final lessons.

First and Third Sessions

- ✓ **Warm up with all your licks. Take your time, have fun!**
- ✓ **Play The Wild Riff.**
- ✓ **Play Your Class Seven song incessantly!**
- ✓ **Finish up with one of your old songs.**

Second Session

- ✓ **Review the best strum and use it to play your Class Three and Class Five songs.**
- ✓ **Review the basic strum and use it to play your Class One and Class Four songs.**
- ✓ **Play your Class Seven song.**

Q: *Dan, is it wrong to practice more than three times a week?*

A: Was Jimi Hendrix British? Is Eric Clapton female? Is Keith Richards attractive?

CLASS SEVEN SONGS
The Best Strum

Since the G-to-C change is so incredibly important in guitar, why don't you warm up with some of the same songs from last week—only this time, try playing the best strum. Again, songs built on good G-to-C-type progressions include **"Bells Ring" by Mazzy Star, "Boss D.J." by Sublime, "Wheat Kings" by The Tragically Hip, "Every Morning" by Sugar Ray** and lots more which you will probably discover for yourself.

The Best G to C Song Ever

⊓ ⊓ ∨ ∨ ⊓ ∨
① + ② ⊕ 3 ⊕ ④ ⊕ etc.
|: G | C :|

The G-C-G-D progression is closely related to the chorus to **Sam Cooke's "Another Saturday Night"** (capo II...it was covered by **Cat Stevens**, too) or the verse to **Van Morrison's "Brown Eyed Girl"** (open). You can also use it to play **"The Lion Sleeps Tonight"** (open, **The Tokens** and others).

In the Jungle

⊓ ⊓ ∨ ∨ ⊓ ∨
① + ② ⊕ 3 ⊕ ④ ⊕ etc.
|: G | C | G | D :|

Below is a two part chord progression to practice your best strums and G to C changes. It is similar to **"Brown Eyed Girl,"** so I challenge you to get a copy of that song and try to adapt the progression to play it.

Brown Eyed Chords

Verse
⊓ ⊓ ∨ ∨ ⊓ ∨
① + ② ⊕ 3 ⊕ ④ ⊕ etc.
: G	C	G	D
G	C	G	D
G	C	G	D
G	C	G	D

Chorus
| C | D | G | Em |
| C | D | G | D :|

CLASS ____ PRACTICE CHART: ______________________________

Your teacher will assign you something great to fill in on this page! (If you're studying this book on your own, then use this page as a worksheet to figure out and write down an entire song you'd like to practice, or just write your own if you prefer.)

RHYTHM: | 1 + 2 + 3 + 4 + |

PRACTICE TAB, LICK or RIFF

T
A
B

CLASS

8

How Great Guitarists Think About Music

~ by Dan Emery of NYC Guitar School ©2009 ~

First, decide what song you will play in class 10!
A and E with pivots.

Before Learning How Great Guitar Players Understand Songs, Learn the Mighty A Chord

GOOD GUITAR PLAYERS are efficient: They leave fingers down when possible. Make a D chord and the LEAVE YOUR FIRST FINGER DOWN while you make a new chord, the A-major chord.

A Major

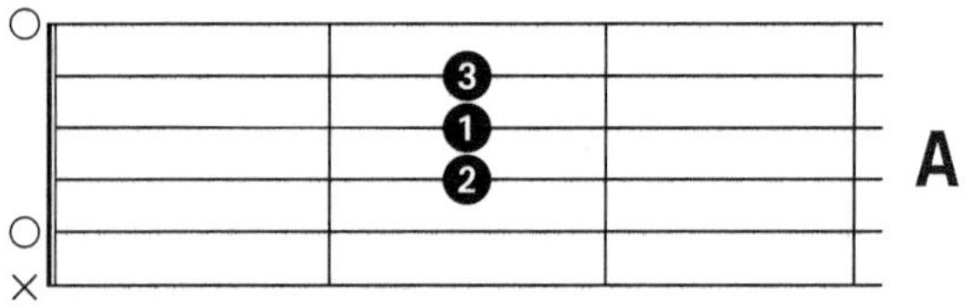

AH, THE A-MAJOR CHORD. Mike Dulak taught it to me, back in Moscow, Idaho. Thanks, Mike, for teaching me my first guitar chord and banjo, too! Note that this is a five-string chord.

You know A7. You know A minor. And now you know A major, which is usually just called "A." You've got a lot of A chords! Did you know that there are many different ways to finger a chord? For example, many good guitarists finger an A chord with their fingers in a row. Try it:

Also A Major

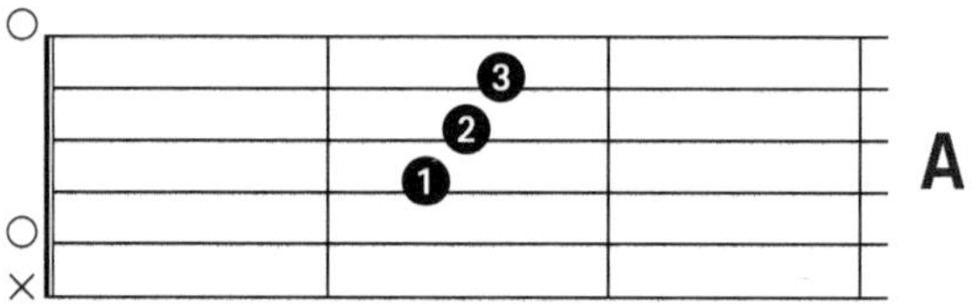

THIS IS A LEGITIMATE WAY to finger an A chord. But it doesn't give as many pivots or set up as many other future chord changes.

A year from now, you may use several different fingerings for each chord you know. Right now, give yourself a strong foundation for future guitar playing by using the first fingering given. Spend a few minutes changing between D and A leaving your first finger down, without counting. When you start to feel comfortable, add the best strum.

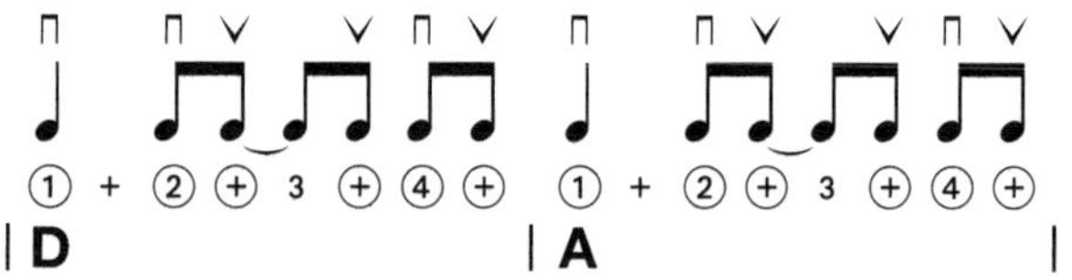

Continue Preparing to Understand Songs with the Mighty E Chord with a SLIDING Pivot

GOOD GUITAR PLAYERS are efficient: They leave fingers down when possible. Make a D chord and then **slide your first finger on the third string** while you make a new chord, the E-major chord. Your fingertip will never leave the third string, even though you are changing frets.

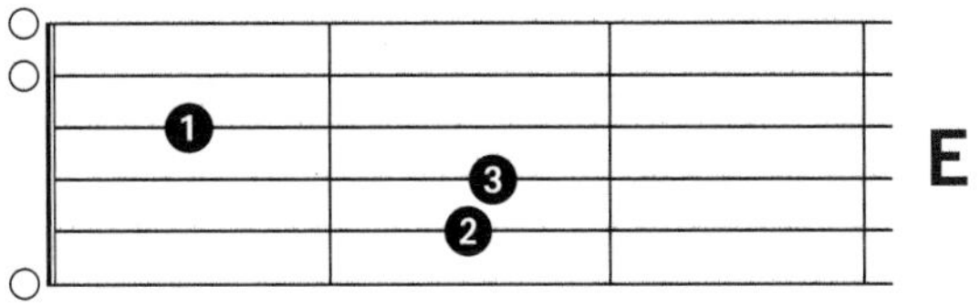

Now change between D and E. Begin with just one strum per measure, and work up to the best strum. **Keep your first finger down!**

⊓ ⊓ V V ⊓ V ⊓ ⊓ V V ⊓ V
① + ② ⊕ 3 ⊕ ④ ⊕ ① + ② ⊕ 3 ⊕ ④ ⊕
𝄆 D | E 𝄇

When you are finished with that, try A to E. Begin with one strum per chord and work up to the best strum again. **Don't pick up your first finger—instead, slide it along the third string.**

⊓ ⊓ V V ⊓ V ⊓ ⊓ V V ⊓ V
① + ② ⊕ 3 ⊕ ④ ⊕ ① + ② ⊕ 3 ⊕ ④ ⊕
𝄆 A | E 𝄇

This progression is used in lots of songs, including "Sympathy For The Devil" by the Rolling Stones and the end of almost every blues song. It is a great progression for trying out your pivot changes. **Leave the first finger down.** Try it out!

𝄆 E | D |
| A | E 𝄇

How Great Guitar Players Think about Music

MUSIC THEORY involves perceiving the patterns in music. You've already done this by noticing that chord progressions usually happen in sets of four or eight. Now you will learn to notice even deeper patterns.

Do you remember our "Wild Riff?" Let's play it a few times:

① + ② + 3 ⊕ ④ + ① + ② + 3 ⊕ ④ +
𝄆 G / C / | D / C / 𝄇

Jimi Hendrix is one of the many great guitarists who played this riff. Incredibly, he did not think of it as "G-G-C-C-D-D-C-C." Instead, he thought of it as a set of **relationships** among chords, which in this particular instance used G, C and D. Whenever he felt like it, he used completely different chords to play the song, and it still sounded right, because he kept the relationship the same. That's what good guitar players do: They see structure and **relationships** in songs where the inexperienced player may see only a set of random chords.

Go to the circus and you'll see lots of parents and kids. When you look at them, you'll immediately identify a set as "probably a mom, a big brother, a little sister" for example. Later you may learn that

THE E MAJOR CHORD
If you ever want to play Johnny Cash songs, you'd better get good at playing E.

THE A MAJOR CHORD
The preferred NYC Guitar School fingering for an A Major may look convoluted, but it makes changing to D and E a snap, because you can use your first finger as a pivot.

their names are Miriam, Elijah and Neoma, and that they are my family—but you don't need to know those specifics to understand the relationships involved. As a human you instinctively sense the connections between people. Now you will learn the relationships between chords.

Q: *Dan, this music-theory stuff sounds hard.*

A: And yet, what you will learn today is shockingly easy given its power and utility.

Begin Learning Music Theory in a Shockingly Easy Manner!

Step one: Can you count on your fingers, starting with your thumb? Try it. Feel free to use the handy guide below. Note that I have used Roman Numerals as well as Arabic Numerals:

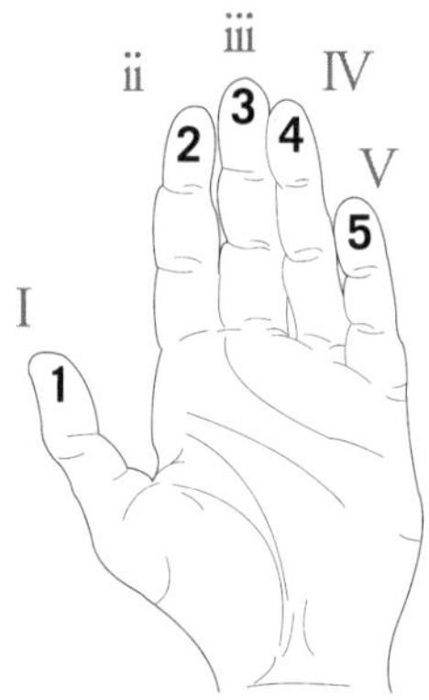

Step two: Can you say the musical alphabet? It is just like the regular alphabet, except that there are only seven letters: A, B, C, D, E, F and G. Whenever you get to "G" you start over with A again. The other wrinkle is that you can start on any letter. Study the following examples:

The musical alphabet starting with A is
A, B, C, D, E, F, G, A, B, C, D, E, F, etc.

The musical alphabet starting with C is
C, D, E, F, G, A, B, C, D, E, F, G, A, etc.

The musical alphabet starting with G is
G, A, B, C, D, E, F, G, A, B, C, D, E, etc.

Continue Learning Music Theory in a Shockingly Easy Manner!

For reasons having to do with the physics of music, any note is strongly related to the fourth and fifth notes following it. This is not a random relationship. These three notes, called the "first note," the "fourth note" and the "fifth note" are caused by vibrations which are mathematically related. They are **in harmony** with each other. In other words, they sound good! Practice counting on your hands as follows:

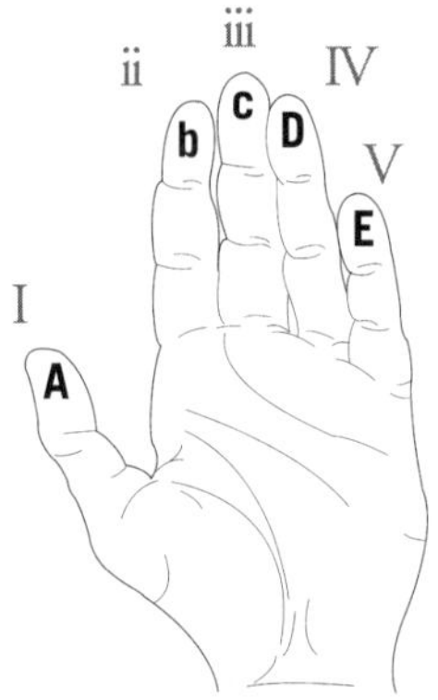

STARTING WITH A

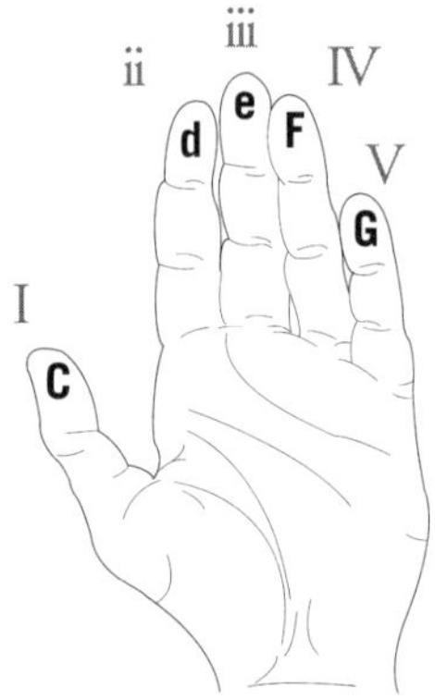

STARTING WITH C

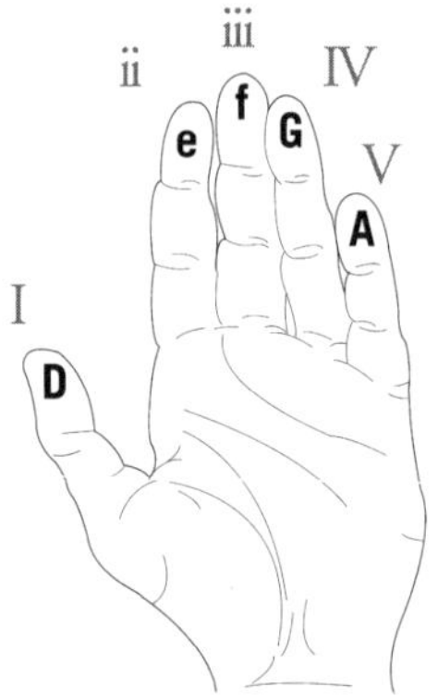

STARTING WITH D

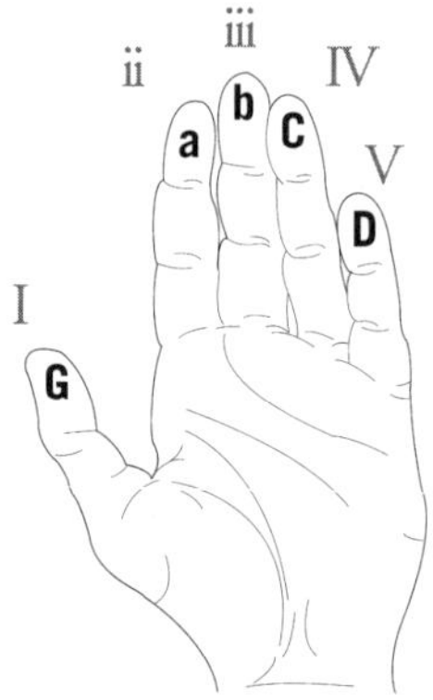

STARTING WITH G

Songs usually start and end on the same chord. This chord can be called the "one" chord, and would be written as a Roman Numeral: I. The other major chords in the song are almost always the IV and the V chords. Because the I chord is so important, it is the **key** to understanding the song. When somebody says "étude in the key of A major" or "blues in the key of A" or "let's do this one in A" they mean that the I chord will be the A.

If we want to do a song in the key of A, what will the other chords be? Refer to the hand above.

In the key of A, the I chord is A, the IV chord is D, and the V chord is E. In textbooks on music theory, this is usually shown with a chart. Fill in the rest of the chart. Feel free to count on your fingers or to refer to the hand diagrams. You probably don't know how to play all these chords. That's OK.

KEY	I Chord	IV Chord	V Chord
A	A	D	E
C	C		
D			
E			
G			

Let's return to Jimi Hendrix and the Wild Riff. Jimi could play it in the key of G just like us. Play it again.

① + ② + 3 ⊕ ④ + ① + ② + 3 ⊕ ④ +
𝄆 G / C / | D / C / 𝄇

But Jimi perceived the chord progression as a relationship which could be played based on any chord. He thought of it as:

① + ② + 3 ⊕ ④ + ① + ② + 3 ⊕ ④ +
𝄆 I / IV / | V / IV / 𝄇

Because he knew music theory, he then played that progression starting with any chord he wanted, for example, the A chord. So how does this song go in the key of A? Fill it in, referring to the Key of A chart as necessary.

KEY	I Chord	IV Chord	V Chord
A	A	D	E

① + ② + 3 ⊕ ④ + ① + ② + 3 ⊕ ④ +
𝄆 I = __ IV = __ | V = __ IV = __ 𝄇

Take your time. Refer to the charts, count on your fingers, and figure out how to transpose (that means "change") the wild riff from the key of G to the key of A. Play it a few times and notice that it definitely still sounds right; the chords are different but the song remains the same!

Q: *Dan, is this all there is to music theory?*

A: No. It just goes on and on and gets more and more complicated—but so what? I've heard that Mozart became frustrated because he couldn't understand everything in a music-theory textbook by the choral music composer Palestrina. Music theory is endless, just like quantum physics is endless. But you don't need to understand the theory of relativity to know that "what goes up must come down." And you don't need to know jazz chord substitutions or counterpoint harmony to know that A, D and E sound good together! At this point we don't need to know about sharps or flats or relative minors or any of a million other things. The best thing you can do to prepare to learn these other concepts later is to pay attention to the I-IV-V theory that we learned today.

Return to Pivots!

Try out one more cool pivot with your new A major chord. This change is to C, and your second finger remains down. Start with single strums per measure and work up to the best strum!

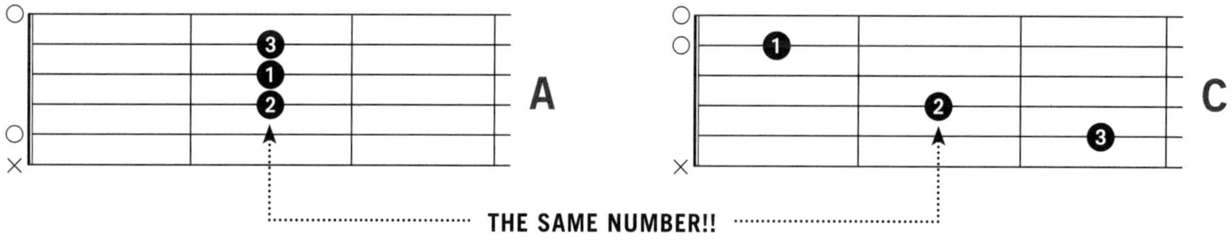

Practice Suggestions for Class Eight

This is an important week of practice! You are nearing the end of the course—this is a vital week for solidifying what you've learned so far, so that you can understand new concepts in the final lessons.

First and Third Sessions

- ✓ Warm up by playing a selection of riffs and licks.
- ✓ Strum through your Class Eight songs.
- ✓ Play your song for Class Ten over and over again. Play it sitting in one chair. Play it sitting in another. Play it singing. Play it without singing. Play it fast. Play it slow. Then practice it for a friend or relative, or record yourself playing it, or play it into the mirror!

Second and Fourth Sessions

- ✓ Warm up with a selection of licks and riffs.
- ✓ Play your song for Class Ten over and over. Play it looking only at your right hand. Play it looking only at your left hand. Play it with your eyes closed.

CONGRATULATIONS ON LEARNING SO MUCH AND PRACTICING SO MUCH!

GOOD GUITARISTS KNOW THAT PLAYING IN RHYTHM IS MOST IMPORTANT!

The secret to playing great rhythm guitar is to move your hand with the beat. Usually this means: ON the beat, strum DOWN. OFF the beat, strum UP.

GOOD GUITARISTS ARE EFFICIENT. LEAVE FINGERS DOWN WHENEVER POSSIBLE —PIVOT, PIVOT, PIVOT!

USE YOUR FINGERTIP TO FRET NOTES, ALMOST BUT NOT QUITE ON THE FRET.

STRUM EFFICIENTLY, USING REST STROKES.

WHEN CHANGING CHORDS, MOVE THE MOST IMPORTANT FINGER FIRST.

ALWAYS PLAY THE OPTIMUM NUMBER OF STRINGS IN A CHORD.

PERCEIVE AND REMEMBER PATTERNS IN MUSIC!

CLASS EIGHT SONGS

More Best Strum plus WILD RIFF w/A-D-E

In the key of A, a I-IV progression would be A to D, which can be found in songs like **"All I Want Is You" by U2** (open) and **"In Between Days" by The Cure** (open) What? Just two chords? Yes—these great songs and many others are written off of just a couple of chords! After all, the essence of great guitar playing is not "lots of chords"—the essence of great guitar playing is LOTS OF EXPRESSION. Listen to "All I Want Is You." The Edge is playing his heart out with two chords—he's strumming them one way, then another. He's fingering them this way, then that way. He's adding a note. He's taking a note away. He can do this because his foundation is so secure—he's thinking of this song as a two-chord vamp and then he's letting his heart take over. As always, download the song or get the CD so that you can soak up the feeling of a great guitar player. Then emulate the feeling. Sure, you don't know everything that the Edge knows about guitar playing—but you know how it feels to be alive and to feel deeply…so play this song like you mean it!

All I Want is A to D

𝄆 A | D 𝄇

The next progression will allow you to sing the "naaaa...naaa...naaa....na na na naaaaa...." part of **The Beatles' "Hey Jude"** (capo V). In open position you can sing along with the **"Seven Bridges Road" by Steve Young** (I'm sure you've heard **The Eagles'** version, or one by **Dolly Parton, Ian Matthews** or **FireHouse**) and especially for us guitar players, the verse to **Guns n' Roses' "Sweet Child o' Mine."** I'm calling the progression "Sweet Chord Changes" in honor of that song.

Sweet Chord Changes

𝄆 D | D | C | C |

| G | G | D | D 𝄇

Improve your A-to-C change with the chord progression below, which is similar to the chorus of **"Sweet Child o' Mine"** and the big jam at the end of **Lynyrd Skynyrd's "Freebird."** Mess around with those songs open (no capo).

Sweet Chorus Changes

𝄆 A | C | D | D |

| A | C | D | D 𝄇

Here's The Wild Riff again, only in the key of A, using A, D and E instead of G, C and D.

The Wild Riff

⊓ ⊓ ⊓ ⊓ ⊓ ⊓ ⊓ ⊓

① + ② + 3 ⊕ ④ + ① + ② + 3 ⊕ ④ +

𝄆 A / D / | E / D / 𝄇

(Here's an extra-credit project: The D-C-G-D progression from the top of the page can be adapted for **"Swingin'" by Tom Petty and The Heartbreakers, "Time Has Come Today" by The Ramones,** and the chorus to **"Angel From Montgomery" by John Prine.** Download one of those songs and see if you can figure out how to play it!)

CLASS ____ PRACTICE CHART: ______________________

Your teacher will assign you something great to fill in on this page! (If you're studying this book on your own, then use this page as a worksheet to figure out and write down an entire song you'd like to practice, or just write your own if you prefer.)

RHYTHM: | 1 + 2 + 3 + 4 + |

PRACTICE TAB, LICK or RIFF

T
A
B

CLASS

9

RHYTHM 102: Mixed Rhythms and Split Measures

~ by Dan Emery of NYC Guitar School ©2009 ~

— CLASS TEN NOTE —

If you are inviting guests to Class Ten next week, ask them to come for the last 15-20 minutes of class. They are welcome to wait in the lounge beforehand. (At the discretion and inclination of the students and teacher, you may wish to spend the bulk of this lesson working on your Class Ten song.)

Mixed Rhythms

THIS LESSON continues to build on your fundamental habit of locking your hand in with the beat, even if you are not actually strumming. Let's play through each of our massively useful rhythms for a moment in order to prepare for mixed rhythms. First, the basic strum:

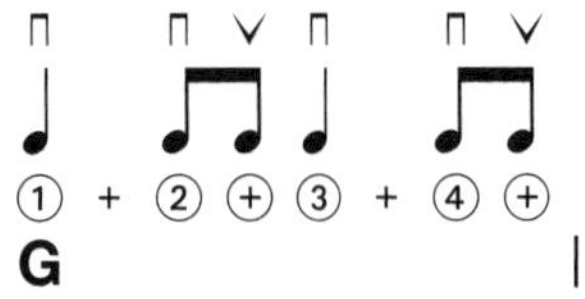

After you've played through the basic strum a few times, review the best strum:

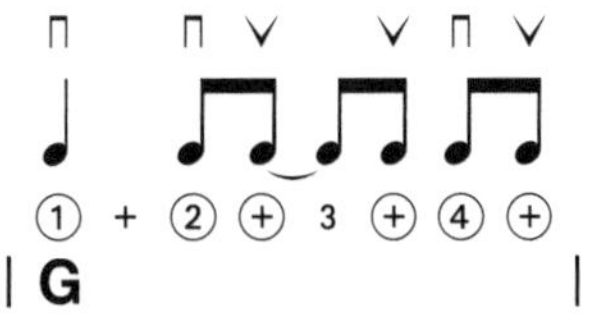

Now you are ready to mix these two rhythms together. On the first measure you will play the best strum, smoothly continuing with the basic strum on the second measure. Remember to **keep your hand moving!** You will be playing a different strum pattern on each measure. Play the following line until you are moderately comfortable and confident with it. The chord remains the same—only the strum is changed!

HERE IS THE BEST STRUM — **HERE IS THE BASIC STRUM**

⊓ ⊓ ∨ ∨ ⊓ ∨ | ⊓ ⊓ ∨ ⊓ ⊓ ∨
① + ② ⊕ 3 ⊕ ④ ⊕ | ① + ② ⊕ ③ + ④ ⊕
|: G | G :|

In a way, this will be easier with a chord change, because it will be easier to hear the two different patterns. Try a pivot change for a few times:

HERE IS THE BEST STRUM — **HERE IS THE BASIC STRUM**

⊓ ⊓ ∨ ∨ ⊓ ∨ | ⊓ ⊓ ∨ ⊓ ⊓ ∨
① + ② ⊕ 3 ⊕ ④ ⊕ | ① + ② ⊕ ③ + ④ ⊕
|: Em | G :|

And now play mixed rhythms with a plant change, D to G. Here I've written the rhythm in notation and without the pick direction, because you remember that on the beat, your hand moves down, and off the beat your hand moves up! (In this class you don't have to read standard rhythm notation—I just put it in now and then so it will soak into you by osmosis and help prepare you for the next course.) Play through this change a bunch of times until you feel comfortable smoothly repeating the line:

Your Sure-Fire Method to Sound Great on Just about Any Song

As you know, some measures of music contain two chords. That means that you will often need to change chords in the middle of a measure. We can call these measures **split measures** because they are split into two chords. Here is a typical progression:

|: D G | A7 :|

What do you do? Well, as a guitarist with ever-greater understanding and skill, you will soon feel that the possibilities are infinite. In the meantime, 99 percent of the time your songs will sound great if you play them with the best strum, except for split measures, which you'll handle with the basic strum. In fact, let's make a note of this:

A great default arrangement for virtually any song is to play all one-chord measures with the best strum, and to play all split measures with the basic strum.

Let's give it a shot. The following two measures can be used to play "La Bamba," "Twist and Shout" and lots of other songs. Play through them until you get modestly comfortable. The D will fall right on the "one" and the G will fall right on the "three".

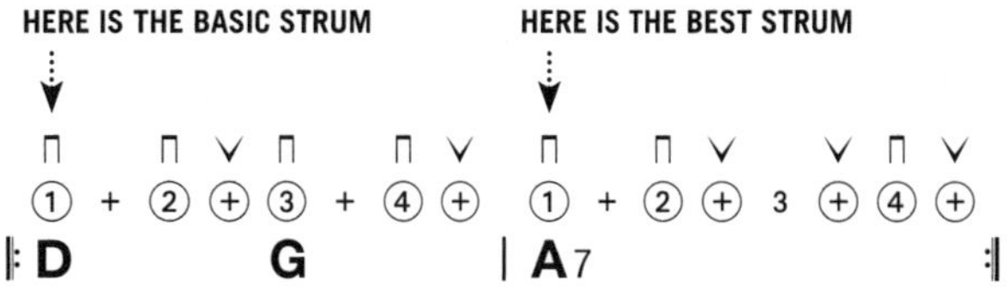

The key, as always, is to **keep your hand moving.** Here's another typical two-measure progression to get comfortable with. It is the chorus for such songs as "Imagine" by the Beatles, "Redemption Song" by Bob Marley and numerous other tunes. I put it down in rhythm notation.

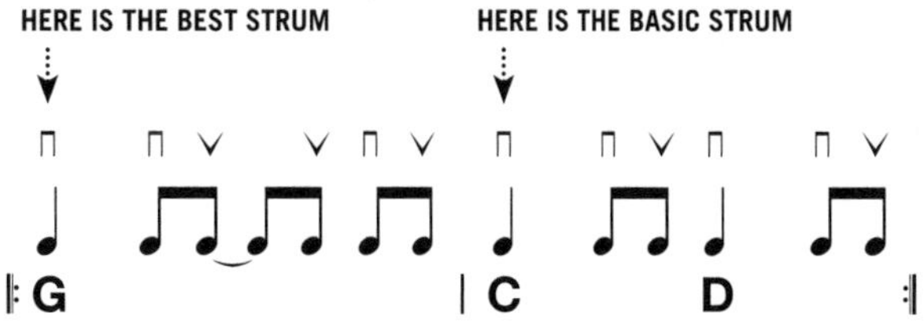

Good guitarists don't just bash away at the guitar with a single uniform strum all the way through a song. They are expressive and flexible. You will be too. Remember this:

A great default arrangement for virtually any song is to play all one-chord measures with the best strum, and to play all split measures with the basic strum.

FUNDAMENTAL HABITS OF A GOOD GUITAR PLAYER

GOOD GUITARISTS KNOW THAT PLAYING IN RHYTHM IS MOST IMPORTANT!

The secret to playing great rhythm guitar is to move your hand with the beat. Usually this means: ON the beat, strum DOWN. OFF the beat, strum UP.

GOOD GUITARISTS ARE EFFICIENT. LEAVE FINGERS DOWN WHENEVER POSSIBLE —PIVOT, PIVOT, PIVOT!

USE YOUR FINGERTIP TO FRET NOTES, ALMOST BUT NOT QUITE ON THE FRET.

STRUM EFFICIENTLY, USING REST STROKES.

WHEN CHANGING CHORDS, MOVE THE MOST IMPORTANT FINGER FIRST.

ALWAYS PLAY THE OPTIMUM NUMBER OF STRINGS IN A CHORD.

PERCEIVE AND REMEMBER PATTERNS IN MUSIC!

Practice Suggestions for Class Nine

First Session

- ✓ Play through your Class Ten song
- ✓ Play lots of other songs.
- ✓ Play your Class Nine song.

Second Session

- ✓ Warm up by playing your small barre licks, then your licks.
- ✓ Play the progressions below incessantly:

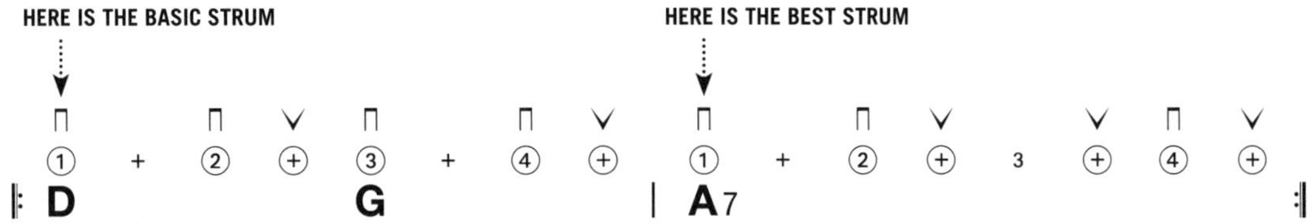

and

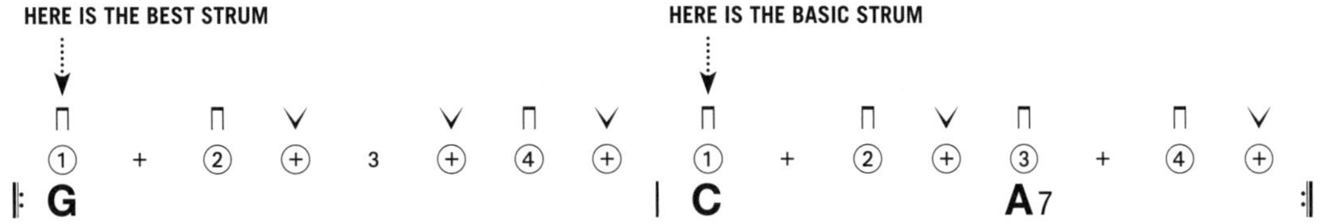

...then play your Class Nine song.

- ✓ Practice your Class Ten song.

Third Session

- ✓ Play your song for Class Ten repeatedly.
- ✓ Play your Class Nine song.
- ✓ Finish with The Wild Riff.

CLASS NINE SONGS

Mixed Rhythms and Split Measures

Congratulations! You now have the chords and strums to have fun and sound good on a large proportion of rock, pop, folk, country, you-name-it guitar songs. As you put together your one-chord-per-measure best strum with your split-measure variant on the basic strum, there will be no stopping you!

Incredible quantities of songs are built off of a two-bar pattern like the one below, with the first measure split between G and C followed by a full measure of D, including **"Twist and Shout" by The Isley Brothers** (The Beatles cover is more well known), **"La Bamba" by Ritchie Valens, "Make Me Lose Control" by Eric Carmen** and **"Stand" by R.E.M.**

```
⊓   ⊓ ∨ ⊓   ⊓ ∨ ⊓   ⊓ ∨   ∨ ⊓ ∨
① + ② ⊕ ③ + ④ ⊕ ① + ② ⊕ 3 ⊕ ④ ⊕
|: G    C       | D             :|
```

Play the same chords in the same order, but with a full measure of G and a split measure of C and D and you have the harmony behind **"Come On Let's Go"** (once again by **Ritchie Valens**) and the choruses to **"Redemption Song" by Bob Marley** and **"Imagine" by John Lennon.**

```
⊓   ⊓ ∨   ∨ ⊓ ∨ ⊓   ⊓ ∨ ⊓   ⊓ ∨
① + ② ⊕ 3 ⊕ ④ ⊕ ① + ② ⊕ ③ + ④ ⊕
|: G            | C     D       :|
```

Here's a more complicated progression for you, mixing best strums and basic strums, in the style of **"Redemption Song."**

Redemption Chords

```
⊓   ⊓ ∨   ∨ ⊓ ∨
① + ② ⊕ 3 ⊕ ④ ⊕ etc.
|: G        | Em       | C        | Am       |
|  G        | Em       | C        | Am       |
|  G        | Em       | C        | Am       |
|  G        | Em       | C        | D    | D |
```

```
⊓   ⊓ ∨   ∨ ⊓ ∨ ⊓   ⊓ ∨ ⊓   ⊓ ∨
① + ② ⊕ 3 ⊕ ④ ⊕ ① + ② ⊕ ③ + ④ ⊕ etc.
| G        | C    D    | G        | C    D    |
| Em       | C    D    | G        | C    D   :|
```

CLASS ____ PRACTICE CHART: ________________________________

Your teacher will assign you something great to fill in on this page! (If you're studying this book on your own, then use this page as a worksheet to figure out and write down an entire song you'd like to practice, or just write your own if you prefer.)

RHYTHM: | 1 + 2 + 3 + 4 + |

PRACTICE TAB, LICK or RIFF

T
A
B

CLASS

10

REVIEW, OPEN CLASS AND GRAND FINALE!

~ by Dan Emery of NYC Guitar School ©2009 ~

{ *CONGRATULATIONS!!* }

CONGRATULATIONS. If you practiced several times a week over the past two and a half months then you are a significantly improved guitar player. You know the most commonly used chords in guitar, you can strum on and off the beat, you can read chord diagrams and tablature, you can play songs, licks and riffs, you can play several of the most important strum patterns in guitar... you have made a tremendous amount of progress, and you deserve to be proud.

I'm writing these words in the Borders bookstore near Madison Square Garden...my table is littered with empty coffee cups, and I've just finished proofing the final layout of this guitar manual, so I'm feeling a sense of accomplishment, too.

I'm pondering the effect of little steps over time. A finished book begins with a few words, and over time, repeated sessions of writing result in what to me is a bit of a miracle—a finished book! And every capable and confident guitar player began as a novice guitar player who knew nothing, but kept playing. Like you. Good job!

At your teachers discretion you may just go right on to get some last minute practice in on your Class Ten performance song. Otherwise, let's review your massive array of new-found guitar skills.

CONGRATULATIONS!
You Know the Most Essential Guitar Chords.

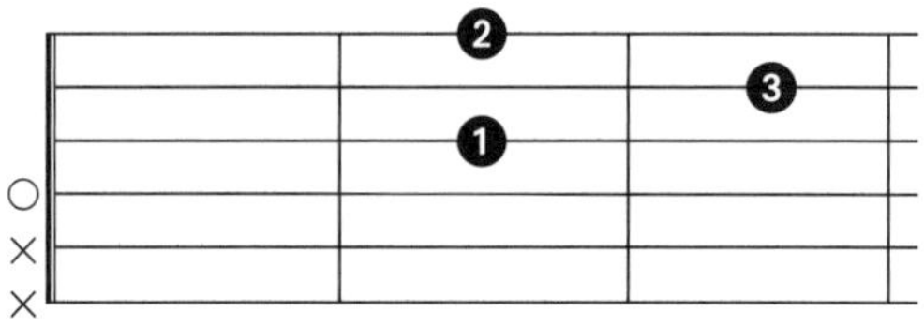

D

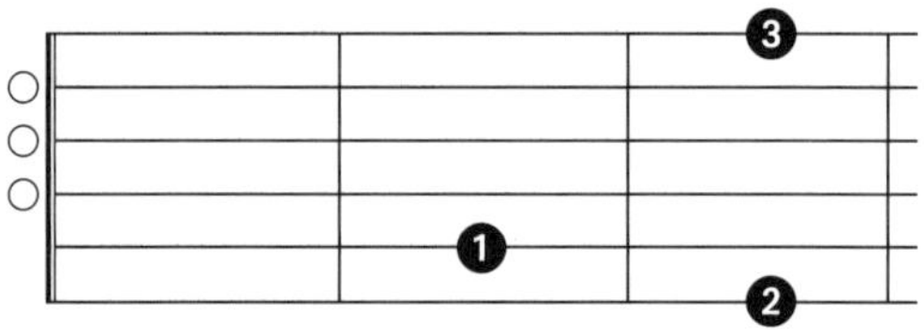

G

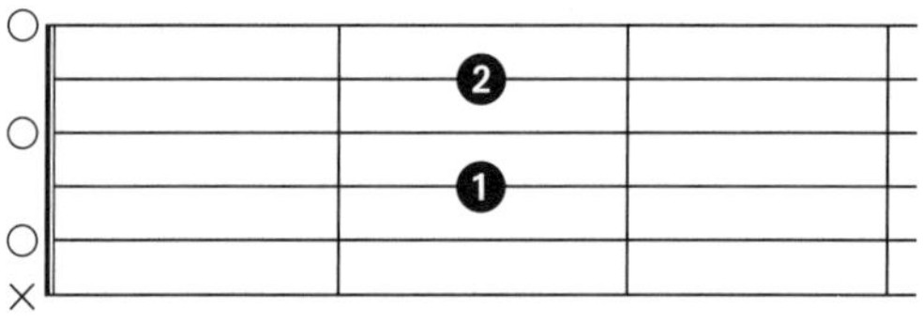

A7

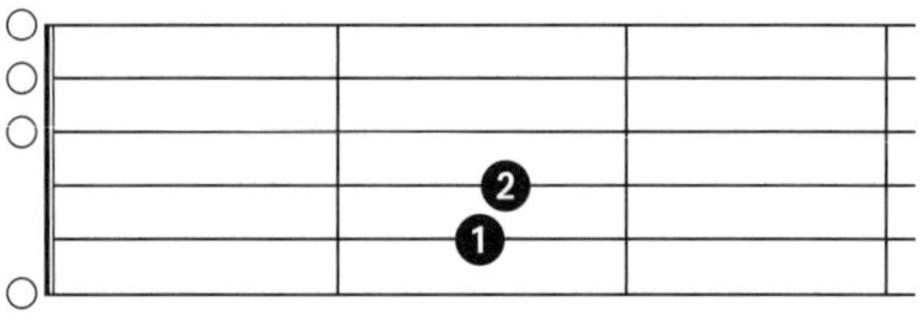

Em

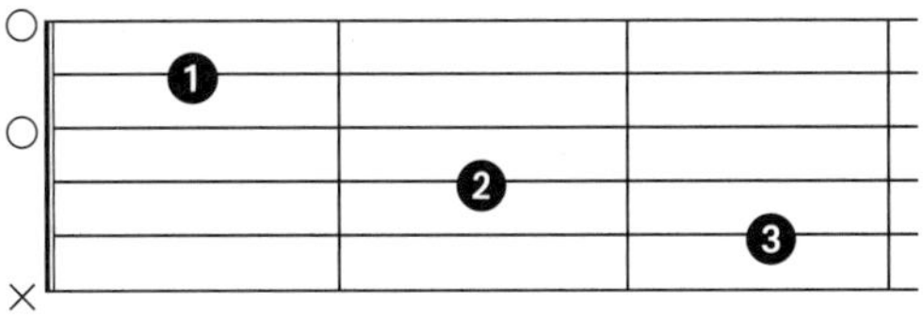

C

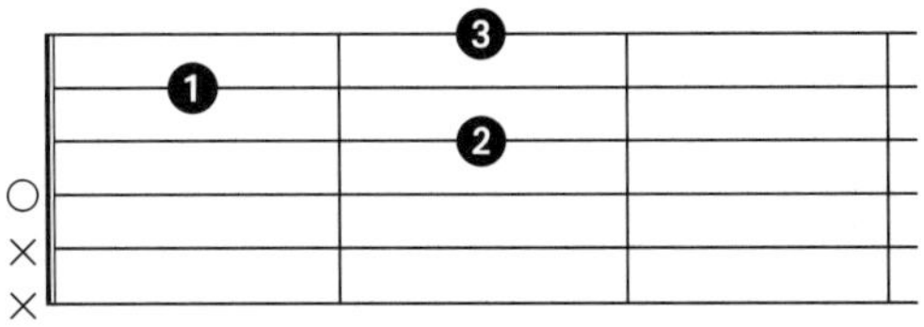

D7

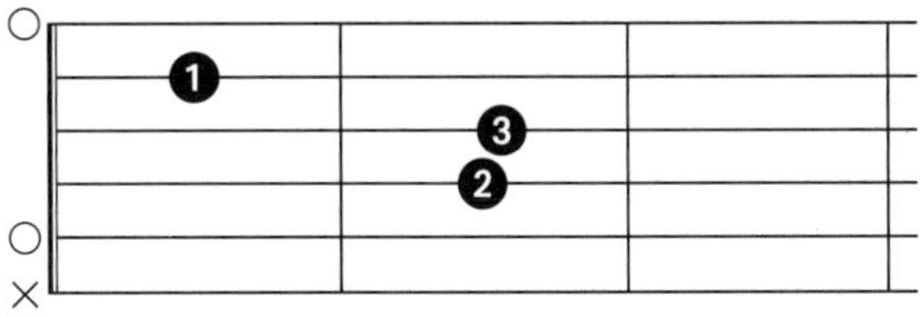

Am

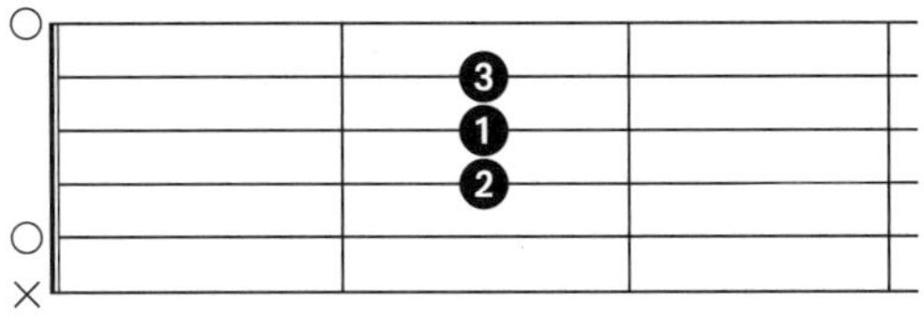

A

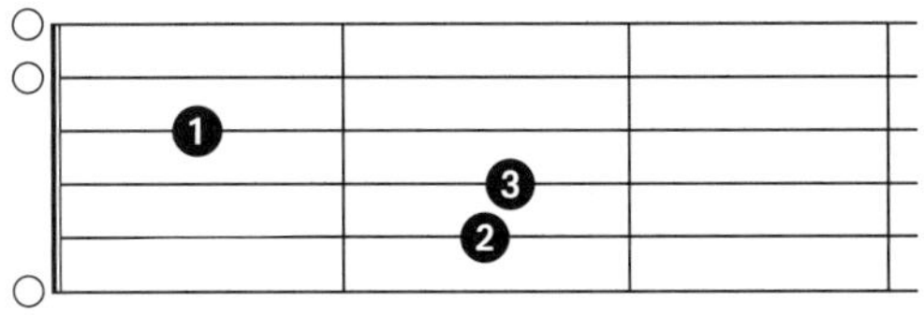

E

Are there more chords? Yes, but you can play thousands of songs with the chords you know. These chords are the most commonly used chords in guitar…and every future chord will be "another chord" instead of "the first chord."

TO MASTER GUITAR PLAYING YOU MUST PLAY YOUR GUITAR!

CONGRATULATIONS!
Rhythm Is Most Important, and You've Learned a Lot of Rhythm!

THE ALTERNATE STRUM:

⊓ V ⊓ V ⊓ V ⊓ V
① ⊕ ② ⊕ ③ ⊕ ④ ⊕ etc.
‖: D A7 | G A7 :‖

RIFFING:

The WILD Riff!

⊓ ⊓ ⊓ ⊓ ⊓ ⊓ ⊓ ⊓
① + ② + 3 ⊕ ④ + ① + ② + 3 ⊕ ④ +
‖: G G C C | D D C C :‖

THE BASIC STRUM:

⊓ ⊓ V ⊓ ⊓ V ⊓ ⊓ V ⊓ ⊓ V
① + ② ⊕ ③ + ④ ⊕ ① + ② ⊕ ③ + ④ ⊕
‖: D | G :‖

THE BEST STRUM:

⊓ ⊓ V V ⊓ V ⊓ ⊓ V V ⊓ V
① + ② ⊕ 3 ⊕ ④ ⊕ ① + ② ⊕ 3 ⊕ ④ ⊕
‖: G | C :‖

MIXED RHYTHMS AND SPLIT MEASURES:

HERE IS THE BASIC STRUM → HERE IS THE BEST STRUM

⊓ ⊓ V ⊓ ⊓ V ⊓ ⊓ V V ⊓ V
① + ② ⊕ ③ + ④ ⊕ ① + ② ⊕ 3 ⊕ ④ ⊕
‖: D G | A7 :‖

HERE IS THE BEST STRUM → HERE IS THE BASIC STRUM

⊓ ⊓ V V ⊓ V ⊓ ⊓ V ⊓ ⊓ V
① + ② ① 3 ⊕ ④ ⊕ ① + ② ⊕ ③ + ④ ⊕
‖: G | C A7 :‖

And how about all your vital habits?

Fundamental Habits of a Good Guitar Player

Good guitarists know that playing in rhythm is most important!

The secret to playing great rhythm guitar is to move your hand with the beat.
Usually this means: ON the beat, strum DOWN. OFF the beat, strum UP.

Good guitarists are efficient. Leave fingers down whenever possible —pivot, pivot, pivot!

Use your fingertip to fret notes, almost but not quite on the fret.

Strum efficiently, using rest strokes.

When changing chords, move the most important finger first.

Always play the optimum number of strings in a chord.

Perceive and remember patterns in music!

To Practice Guitar or ANYTHING Successfully:

- ✓ Practice accurately. *Festina Lente* ("hurry slowly"). When you practice guitar, practice accurately to create correct patterns in your mind and body.

- ✓ Practice guitar regularly!

> *The heights by great men reached and kept,*
> *Were not attained by sudden flight.*
> *But they, while their companions slept,*
> *Were toiling upwards in the night.*

- ✓ Practice effectively. "If something is worth doing, it is worth doing well." Pay attention to what you are doing.

Dear NYC Guitar School Student—

Congratulations on completing Guitar for Absolute Beginners at NYC Guitar School. In order to finish this class, you've needed to fulfill a commitment to yourself to attend class and to practice. This is a big accomplishment as a guitar player and as a human.

In this class you learned the fundamental habits, chords and rhythms of a good guitar player. You can build on this knowledge over a lifetime of playing. If you would like more formal study we would be privileged to continue helping you in your progress. The next class, Guitar for Near Beginners, covers the fundamentals of expression and tone, as well as adding more rhythms, chords and songs.

Thank you for taking a class at NYC Guitar School. Your teacher, our entire staff and I appreciate the opportunity to be part of your life.

Congratulations on deciding to PLAY GUITAR!

Sincerely,

Dan Emery
Founder, New York City Guitar School

CLASS ____ PRACTICE CHART: ______________________________

Your teacher will assign you something great to fill in on this page! (If you're studying this book on your own, then use this page as a worksheet to figure out and write down an entire song you'd like to practice, or just write your own if you prefer.)

RHYTHM: | 1 + 2 + 3 + 4 + |

PRACTICE TAB, LICK or RIFF

T
A
B

CLASS ____ PRACTICE CHART: ______________________________

Your teacher will assign you something great to fill in on this page! (If you're studying this book on your own, then use this page as a worksheet to figure out and write down an entire song you'd like to practice, or just write your own if you prefer.)

RHYTHM: | 1 + 2 + 3 + 4 + |

PRACTICE TAB, LICK or RIFF

T
A
B

WANT MORE?

Visit New York City Guitar School.
Take the 1 2 3 A C E LIRR to Penn Station or
the B D N Q R F M PATH to Herald Square.
Walk downtown to 30th Street.
We're on the 11th floor of the Recording and Rehearsal Arts Building at
251 West 30th Street, between 7th and 8th Avenue.
Come on by!

View a complete schedule of upcoming classes on
the web at www.NYCGuitarSchool.com.

For more books and special pricing for teachers and schools, contact Jen
at info@NYCGuitarSchool.com or call 646-485-7244.

CANDID PHOTO OF THE AUTHOR, DAN EMERY

Here I am with the tools of my trade—
guitar, dry erase marker and white board.
I really enjoy teaching guitar.